POP
MASTER

www.penguin.co.uk

Also by Phil Swern and Neil Myners

ULTIMATE POPMASTER

POP MASTER

THE NATION'S FAVOURITE POP MUSIC QUIZ

PHIL SWERN AND NEIL MYNERS

bantam

Penguin Random House, One Embassy Gardens, 8 Viaduct Gardens,
London SW11 7BW
www.penguin.co.uk

Transworld is part of the Penguin Random House group of companies
whose addresses can be found at global.penguinrandomhouse.com

First published in Great Britain in 2024 by Bantam
an imprint of Transworld Publishers

A CIP catalogue record for this book
is available from the British Library.

ISBN 9780857505767

Designed by Bobby Birchall, Bobby&Co.
Printed and bound in Great Britain by Clays Ltd, Elcograf S.p.A.

The authorized representative in the EEA is Penguin Random House Ireland,
Morrison Chambers, 32 Nassau Street, Dublin D02 YH68.

Penguin Random House is committed to a sustainable
future for our business, our readers and our planet. This book is made from
Forest Stewardship Council® certified paper.

To all the PopMasters out there.

CONTENTS

ABOUT THE AUTHORS

PHIL SWERN

Best regarded for building one of the biggest private record collections in the world, Phil 'The Collector' Swern has, in his own right, achieved over a dozen entries in *The Guinness Book of Hit Singles* as a record producer with acts such as The Pearls, R & J Stone and The Seashells. In the mid-eighties, Phil collaborated as a writer and performer on Capital's *You Ain't Heard Nothing Yet* and later helped set up the Capital Gold Network. He produced *Pick of the Pops* for Radio 1 in the late 1980s and early 1990s, and has produced the show for Radio 2 since 1997. Phil also co-writes Ken Bruce's daily pop quiz PopMaster, for which he has compiled several successful bestselling books.

NEIL MYNERS

Having studied music to degree and postgrad levels, since 1995 Neil has produced BBC Radio 2's coverage of Paul McCartney's return to the Cavern, the BRIT Awards and the Ivor Novello Awards. He was both music programmer and producer on Richard Allinson's Sony-award-winning late-night show for the network and has been recognized for his work with Bob Harris and WBBC on the documentaries *The Sandy Denny Story* and *The Day John Met Paul*. Neil has written daily questions for PopMaster since 2003 and has continued on the team with Ken's move to Greatest Hits Radio. This book is his sixth collaboration with Phil Swern.

KEN BRUCE

Ken Bruce was born and raised in Glasgow, where he trained and worked as a chartered accountant before he began his broadcasting career in the mid-1970s in hospital radio in Scotland. In 1977 he began working for the BBC as a staff announcer for Radio 4 Scotland, then became one of the original presenters of *Nightbeat*. In 1985 Bruce left Radio Scotland to replace Terry Wogan on Radio 2's *Breakfast Show*, followed by a variety of slots on Radio 2, including the mid-morning slot from 1992 until 2023. It was on this show in 1996 that the daily PopMaster quiz was first introduced with an expected run of just a few months, but its immense popularity has made it an iconic feature of British radio, now still going strong on Ken's mid-morning show on Greatest Hits Radio. PopMaster is a firm fan favourite on radio and has now been turned into a successful TV show broadcast on Channel 4 and More 4.

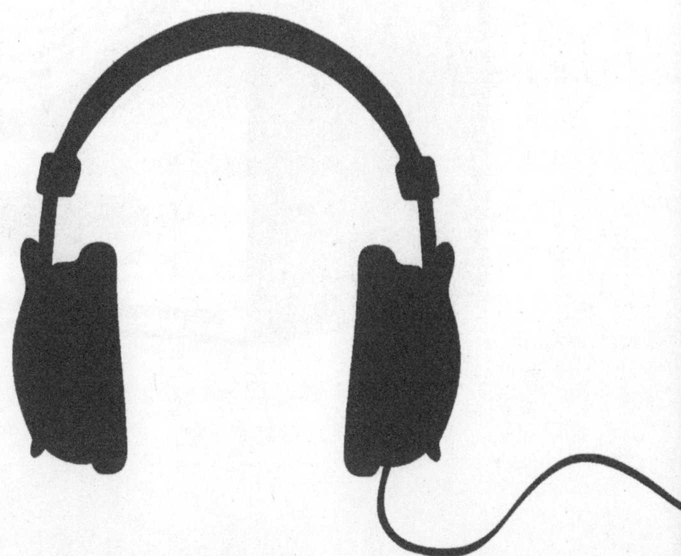

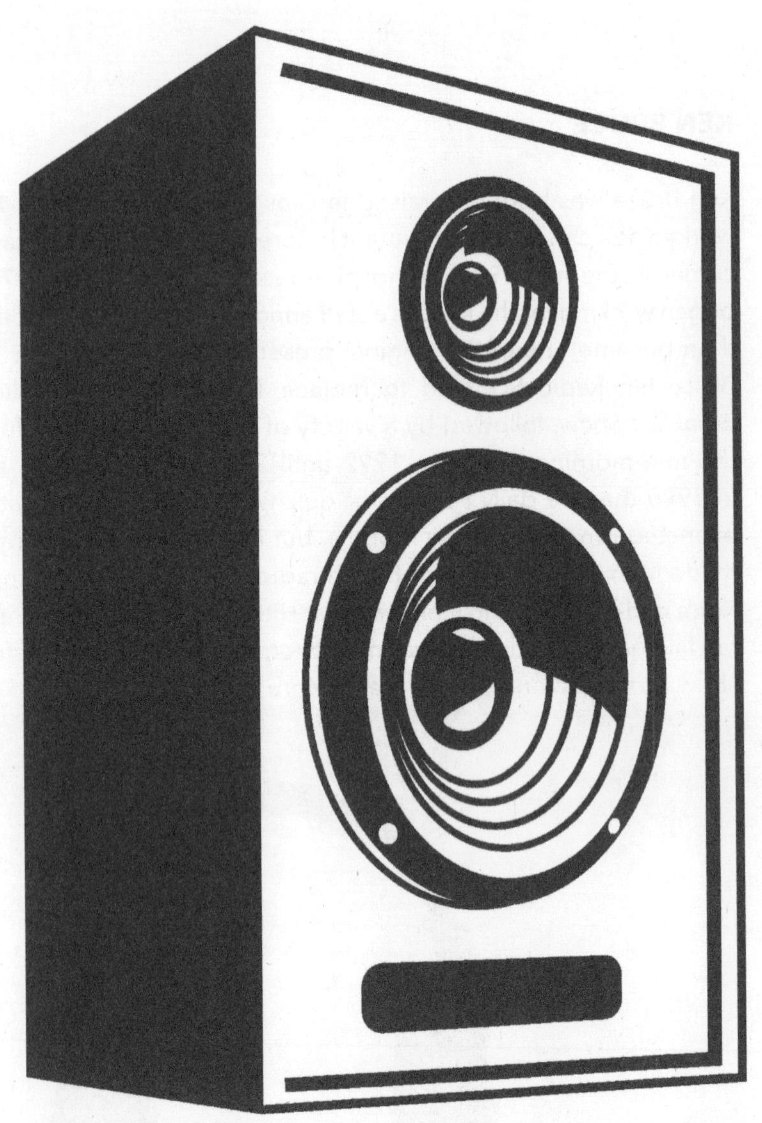

FOREWORD

When I think back to 1996, when PopMaster first appeared on my daily BBC Radio 2 morning show, I can't begin to tell you how thrilled I am that not only is the quiz still running on Greatest Hits Radio, but it has also been turned into a TV show. This is thanks to Jo Street at Channel 4 along with 12 Yard Productions, who had great faith in the project, and the constant nagging and persistence of my co-creator, Phil Swern, to take it to the small screen.

Over the years, the PopMaster radio quiz has become bigger and better, resulting in what has now been recognized as one of the most listened-to thirty minutes of weekday morning radio in the UK. It has also taken on a life of its own with its catchphrase, 'One Year Out', being shouted at me by quizzers as I walk down the road.

In 2020, Penguin Random House published *Ultimate PopMaster* and I am thrilled they have commissioned this second book that you now hold in your hands. I know that much hard work has gone into compiling the questions to make it the best volume yet!

I really hope you enjoy playing along as you turn the pages, all set by our regular question setters, Neil Myners and Phil ('The Collector') Swern – and if you're flicking through a copy in a bookshop then be kind to us and go and make the purchase – you know it makes sense!

Don't forget to join me every weekday morning at 10.30 a.m. on Greatest Hits Radio to hear the quiz, and keep an eye out in the TV listings to catch up on the TV version. You never know, one day you may become one of the lucky ones to become a contestant on a future show.

KEN BRUCE

POPMASTER

Welcome to PopMaster, the nation's favourite pop music quiz. The questions on the following pages cover a whole range of chart acts - from 'East End Boys' to 'West End Girls' and from 'Band(s) On The Run' to artists 'Ridin' Solo'.

There's something for everyone - from a smattering of easy questions to get you in the mood, right through to our devious Champions level, which might well have you tugging on the toggles of your musical anorak. The book is divided into sections, beginning with our General PopMaster. This covers music from the 1950s right through to the 2020s. It's followed by Pick 'n' Mix - thirty sets of questions with different themes. Either work your way through them or choose your favourites.

We then come to The Golden Years, three sections, each concentrating on a different decade, the 1970s, 1980s and 1990s. In each of these sections you'll find ten sets of questions that cover the entire decade, followed by ten slightly trickier sets that each focus on a particular year, and finally, five sets about five successful acts that made their chart debuts in the given decade. The questions, though, cover the whole of their musical careers.

Our Champions section follows. For those of you who are regular listeners to the radio version of the quiz, you'll know that some of these questions can be fiendishly difficult. And to round things off? Well it wouldn't be PopMaster without the danger of being 'One Year Out'!

Answers can be found over the page - for example, if you're looking for the answers to PopMaster 1, they will be underneath the questions of PopMaster 2, and so on. Also, you'll find the occasional nugget of music trivia alongside some of the answers.

We hope you enjoy this latest book. It's been good fun writing it, so hopefully it'll be good fun reading it. But if any of the questions have you tearing your hair out, blame it on the boogie, the bossa nova, the bassline, the rain or the weatherman, but don't blame us. We're just the (paperback) writers!

PHIL SWERN AND NEIL MYNERS

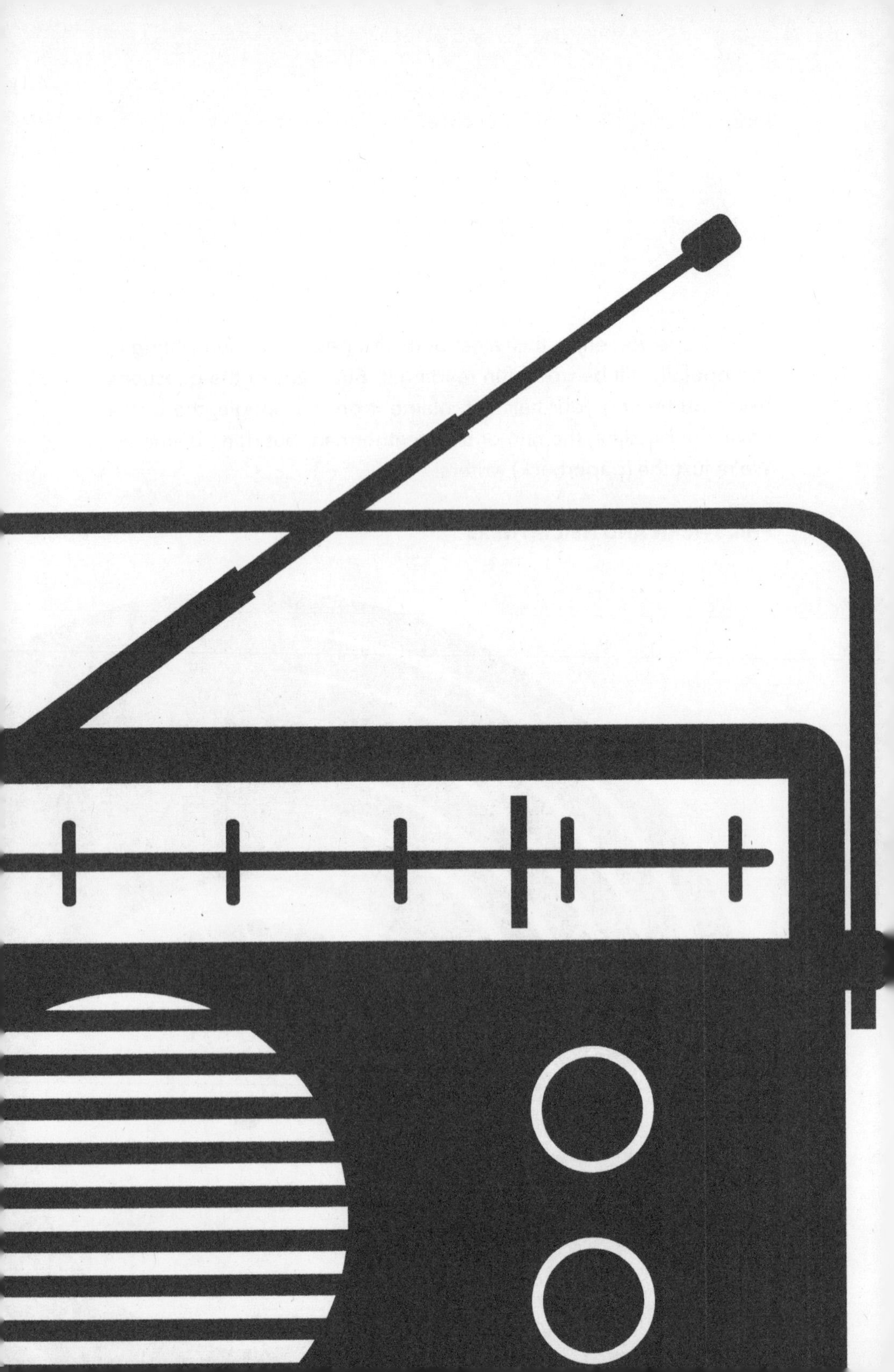

GENERAL POPMASTER

Just to get you warmed up – here are forty sets of questions covering the charts from the 1950s through to the 2020s.

POPMASTER 1

1 'Ticket To Ride' was a number one single in 1965 for which group?

2 Maroon 5's number one debut album in the noughties was called *Songs About* _____ who?

3 The Mike of Mike and the Mechanics first reached the charts in the seventies as guitarist in another group. Who is he and what is the name of that group?

4 Known as bubblegum pop, the 1910 Fruitgum Company had a Top 3 hit in 1968 with which song?

5 Bryan 'Dexter' Holland is the lead singer with the American rock band that reached number one in 1999 with 'Pretty Fly (For A White Guy)'. What is the name of the band?

6. a-ha's second hit single is also the group's only number one in the UK. What is it called?

7. The songs 'Down Boy' and 'Naughty Girl' were both hit singles in 2002 for which one-time *Neighbours* actor?

8. Complete the title of this 1992 Top 20 single by Del Amitri. 'Always The ____' what?

9. What instrument did Rodney Franklin play on his 1980 Top 10 instrumental hit 'The Groove'?

10. In 2023, *Memento Mori* was a Top 3 album for a group whose debut LP *Speak And Spell* was a Top 10 hit 42 years earlier. Can you name the group?

ANSWERS ON NEXT SPREAD

POPMASTER 2

1. What annual sporting event provided Kraftwerk with the title of a Top 40 hit in both 1983 and 1984?

2. Zager & Evans reached number one in 1969 with a song subtitled '(Exordium & Terminus)'. What is its full title?

3. 'Ready For the Weekend' was a Top 3 single in 2009 for which Scottish DJ and producer?

4. According to the 1974 hit for Sparks, who or what should you 'Never Turn Your Back On _____'?

5. Billie Eilish reached number one in 2020 with her theme song to which James Bond film?

6 'Too Lost In You' was a Top 10 single at the end of 2003 for which girl group?

7 Lord Rockingham's XI spent three weeks at number one in the late fifties with which single?

8 'Sing A Happy Song', 'It's Been So Long' and 'I Ain't Lyin'' were all hits in 1975 for which singer?

9 Beginning with the earliest, put these three songs by Kate Bush in the order they were originally hits. 'Rubberband Girl', 'King Of The Mountain' and 'Sat In Your Lap'?

10 *Performance And Cocktails* is the title of a 1999 number one album for which Welsh group?

ANSWERS TO POPMASTER 1

1. The Beatles 2. *Songs About Jane* 3. Mike Rutherford, Genesis 4. 'Simon Says' 5. The Offspring 6. 'The Sun Always Shines On TV' 7. Holly Valance 8. 'Always The Last To Know' 9. Piano 10. Depeche Mode

POPMASTER 3

1. What was the title of the 1981 number one duet by Queen and David Bowie?

2. 'Sweet About Me' was a Top 10 single in 2008 for Gabriella who?

3. Which group reached the charts in 1992 with the singles 'Old Red Eyes Is Back', 'Bell Bottomed Tear' and 'We Are Each Other'?

4. Gilbert O'Sullivan had two number ones in the seventies. 'Clair' in 1972, but which song in 1973?

5. Which band had Top 3 hits in the mid-sixties with 'For Your Love', 'Heart Full Of Soul' and 'Shapes Of Things'?

6 What shared three-word song title gave different Top 10 hits to The Human League in 1981 and Madonna in 1986?

7 Which British female vocal group had Top 10 singles in the nineties called 'Someday', 'I Am Blessed' and 'Angel of Mine'?

8 What is the one-word title of the 2005 number one single by Gorillaz?

9 'I Don't Feel Like Dancin'' spent a month at number one in 2006 for which group?

10 In the sixties, Graham Nash, Tony Hicks, Allan Clarke and Bobby Elliott were all members of which group?

ANSWERS TO POPMASTER 2

1. 'Tour de France' (No. 22 in 1983, No. 24 in 1984) 2. 'In The Year 2525 (Exordium & Terminus)' 3. Calvin Harris 4. 'Never Turn Your Back On Mother Earth' 5. *No Time To Die* 6. Sugababes 7. 'Hoots Mon' (re-released in 1993, spending one week at No. 60) 8. George McCrae 9. 'Sat In Your Lap' (1981), 'Rubberband Girl' (1993), 'King Of The Mountain' (2005) 10. Stereophonics

POPMASTER 4

1. 'Caroline' is the title of a 1973 Top 5 song by which band?

2. Vanessa Paradis made her chart debut in 1988 with which Top 3 song?

3. Prior to his solo career, Bernard Butler had reached the charts in the early nineties as guitarist with which band?

4. Tracey Thorn and Ben Watt have had hit singles and albums recording as which duo?

5. KC and the Sunshine Band first reached the charts in 1974 with which Top 10 song?

6 Under what name did Trevor Horn and Geoff Downes have hits in 1980 with the songs 'The Plastic Age' and 'Clean Clean'?

7 What is Fat Les's curry of choice according to the title of the 1998 Top 3 single?

8 Mumford & Sons reached the charts in 2009 with the song 'Little _____ Man'?

9 Which band, formed on the Isle of Wight in the late seventies, had hits in the eighties with 'Micro-Kid', 'The Sun Goes Down (Living It Up)' and 'Leaving Me Now'?

10 Oleta Adams reached the Top 5 in the early nineties with a song written by Brenda Russell. What is it called?

ANSWERS TO POPMASTER 3

1. 'Under Pressure' 2. Gabriella Cilmi 3. The Beautiful South 4. 'Get Down' 5. The Yardbirds 6. 'Open Your Heart' 7. Eternal 8. 'Dare' 9. Scissor Sisters (released in some countries as 'I Don't Feel Like Dancing') 10. The Hollies (Graham Nash left in 1968)

POPMASTER 5

1 Cilla Black had both of her number ones in 1964. The first was 'Anyone Who Had A Heart'. What was the second?

2 Which group was 'Turning Japanese', according to the title of their 1980 Top 3 hit?

3 Who had both a Top 10 single and album in 2001 called 'Scream If You Wanna Go Faster'?

4 Which song by The Doors reached the Top 40 in both 1971 and 1976?

5 'Sight For Sore Eyes' was a Top 10 single in 1994 for which chart act?

6 Bros had a Top 3 hit in 1988 called 'Drop The ________' what?

7 'Money On My Mind' was number one in 2014 for which singer?

8 What was the title of the only solo Top 10 single achieved by Scott Walker in the sixties?

9 The song 'Home And Dry' was Top 20 in 2002 for which duo?

10 Beginning with the earliest, can you put these three Top 10 songs by Erasure in the order they were originally hits. 'Run To The Sun', 'Breathe' and 'Drama!'?

ANSWERS TO POPMASTER 4

1. Status Quo 2. 'Joe Le Taxi' 3. Suede 4. Everything but the Girl 5. 'Queen Of Clubs' 6. The Buggles 7. 'Vindaloo' 8. 'Little Lion Man' 9. Level 42 10. 'Get Here'

POPMASTER 6

1 What '_____ Runs Out' according to the title of OneRepublic's Top 3 song in 2014?

2 Who was the lead singer with INXS until his death in 1997?

3 Chris Farlowe reached number one in 1966 with his version of which Mick Jagger and Keith Richards song?

4 Which group took the Rolling Stones' 'Sympathy For The Devil' into the Top 10 in 1995?

5 In 1986, the song 'What Have You Done For Me Lately' became the first Top 10 single for which singer?

6 The solo career of Simon Webbe from Blue began with two Top 5 singles in 2005. 'Lay Your Hands' was one of these. What was the other called?

7 Which group's chart debut came with the 1973 Top 20 single 'Crazy'?

8 What '_____ Girls' did Adam and the Ants sing about on the group's 1982 hit?

9 What is the stage name of singer-songwriter Michael Rosenberg, who spent over three months in the Top 10 in 2013 with his song 'Let Her Go'?

10 Which 1963 Top 5 single by The Crystals was a hit for the group again, when it reached the Top 20 in 1974?

ANSWERS TO POPMASTER 5

1. 'You're My World' 2. The Vapors 3. Geri Halliwell 4. 'Riders On The Storm' 5. M People 6. 'Drop The Boy' 7. Sam Smith 8. 'Joanna' 9. Pet Shop Boys 10. 'Drama!' (1989), 'Run To The Sun' (1994), 'Breathe' (2005)

POPMASTER 7

1. The song 'Do You Know The Way To San Jose' was Top 10 in 1968 for which singer?

2. Enigma had its only number one in January 1991 with which single?

3. Who played 'Russian Roulette' on her 2009 Top 3 song?

4. Which George Harrison song gave Steve Harley & Cockney Rebel a Top 10 hit in 1976?

5. The single 'Wunderbar' reached the Top 20 in 1981 for which chart act?

6 What was 'Always Breaking ____' according to the title of Belinda Carlisle's Top 10 single in 1996?

7 Who was 'Levitating' on her 2020 Top 5 song?

8 Released in 1983 and containing the singles 'Every Breath You Take', 'Wrapped Around Your Finger' and 'King Of Pain', what is the title of the final studio album by The Police?

9 The American singer O.C. Smith had a Top 3 single in the late sixties with 'Son Of Hickory Holler's Tramp'. He returned to the Top 40 in 1977 with his only other UK hit. What was it called?

10 'The Shock Of The Lightning' was a Top 3 single in 2008 for which group?

ANSWERS TO POPMASTER 6

1. 'Love Runs Out' 2. Michael Hutchence 3. 'Out Of Time' 4. Guns N' Roses 5. Janet Jackson 6. 'No Worries' 7. Mud 8. 'Deutscher Girls' (released by former record label on the back of the group's success) 9. Passenger 10. 'Da Doo Ron Ron'

POPMASTER 8

1 In 2022, Harry Styles had a Top 3 song called 'Music For A ____' what?

2 'Crazy Water', 'Bite Your Lip (Get Up And Dance)' and 'Ego' were three of the smaller Top 40 hits in the seventies for one of the decade's biggest artists. Name the artist.

3 What is the two-word title of the 1993 Top 3 chart debut by Chaka Demus and Pliers?

4 The song 'Only Love Can Hurt Like This' was Top 10 in 2014 for which singer?

5 Released in 1985, which multi-platinum studio album by Phil Collins included the hit singles 'Sussudio', 'One More Night' and 'Take Me Home'?

6 Who or what was 'Distant ____' according to the title of Jim Reeves' 1966 number one?

7 The song 'Two Can Play That Game' was Top 3 in the mid-nineties for which American singer?

8 The duo Baccara had two Top 40 hits, the number one 'Yes Sir, I Can Boogie' in 1977 and a Top 10 follow-up in 1978. What is the title of this second hit?

9 'Spanish' is the title of a 2003 Top 10 single for which singer?

10 Of the thirteen Top 40 hits in the sixties for Dave Dee, Dozy, Beaky, Mick and Tich, only one of them got to number one. What is it called?

ANSWERS TO POPMASTER 7

1. Dionne Warwick 2. 'Sadness Part 1' (In mainland Europe it was spelled 'Sadeness Part 1') 3. Rihanna 4. 'Here Comes The Sun' 5. Tenpole Tudor 6. 'Always Breaking My Heart' 7. Dua Lipa 8. *Synchronicity* 9. 'Together' 10. Oasis

POPMASTER 9

1. What type of '_____ Vibrations' did The Beach Boys sing about on the group's 1966 number one?

2. The song 'Time (Clock Of The Heart)' was Top 3 in 1982 for which group?

3. Which song spent three weeks at number one for No Doubt in 1997?

4. One half of Savage Garden had solo hits in 2002 called 'Insatiable', 'Strange Relationship' and 'I Miss You'. Who is he?

5. What late sixties instrumental number one by Fleetwood Mac nearly reached the top again, when it was re-issued in 1973 and peaked at number two?

6 'Superheroes' was the title of a Top 3 single in 2014 for which Irish group?

7 The chart act Freak Power had its biggest hit in 1995 with which Top 3 single?

8 Known as the UK's 'King of Skiffle', who had a hit in 1956 with 'Rock Island Line'?

9 American soul trio The Hues Corporation had both of their hit singles in 1974. 'Rock The Boat' was the first. What was the second?

10 The songs 'Candy' and 'Pencil Full Of Lead' were Top 20 hits in 2009 for which Scottish singer-songwriter?

ANSWERS TO POPMASTER 8

1. 'Music For A Sushi Restaurant' 2. Elton John 3. 'Tease Me' 4. Paloma Faith 5. *No Jacket Required* 6. 'Distant Drums' 7. Bobby Brown 8. 'Sorry, I'm a Lady' 9. Craig David 10. 'The Legend Of Xanadu'

POPMASTER 10

1. The Undertones first reached the charts in 1978 with which song?

2. Who was the vocalist on Mark Ronson's 2007 Top 3 version of the Zutons' song 'Valerie'?

3. What type of '____ Sunday' did The Monkees sing about on the group's 1967 hit single?

4. The songs 'Happy Ever After' in 1988 and '(Love Moves In) Mysterious Ways' in 1992 were both Top 40 hits for which singer-songwriter?

5. Who did George Ezra 'Blame It On ____' according to the title of his 2014 Top 10 song?

6. 'Rain On Your Parade' was a Top 20 single in 2008 for which Welsh-born singer?

7 In February 1974, three songs that began with the word 'Teenage' were in the Top 20 at the same time. One was The Sweet's Top 3 hit 'Teenage Rampage'. What were the other two, and who recorded them?

8 The songs 'Take That Situation', 'Warning Sign' and 'Love All Day' were all Top 40 hits in the first half of the eighties for which artist?

9 Prior to her solo career, Dusty Springfield had a run of hits in the early sixties as a member of The Springfields, two of which reached the Top 10. Can you name either of these two?

10 Which chart act was 'Walking On The Milky Way' and into the Top 20 in 1996?

ANSWERS TO POPMASTER 9

1. 'Good Vibrations' 2. Culture Club 3. 'Don't Speak' 4. Darren Hayes 5. 'Albatross' (held off No. 1 in 1973 by 10cc's 'Rubber Bullets') 6. The Script 7. 'Turn On, Tune In, Cop Out' (had originally been released in 1993) 8. Lonnie Donegan 9. 'Rockin' Soul' 10. Paolo Nutini

POPMASTER 11

1. What 2020 number one duet was recorded by Lady Gaga and Ariana Grande?

2. The songs 'Real Real Real', 'Right Here, Right Now' and 'The Devil You Know' were all hits in the first half of the nineties for which group?

3. What 1979 Top 3 song by The Three Degrees has the same title as a 1980 number one for Barbra Streisand?

4. Released in 1967, who had a number one in early 1968 singing about 'The Ballad Of Bonnie And Clyde'?

5. Dead Or Alive first reached the Top 40 in 1984 with a cover of a disco hit from the mid-seventies. What is the song?

6. Under what name did sisters Karen and Shelly Poole have eight Top 40 hits between 1996 and 2001?

7. What 2003 single by Outkast spent a total of three months in the Top 10 and reached its Top 3 peak in the early months of 2004?

8. 'Wasteland', 'Severina' and 'Tower Of Strength' were all singles in the second half of the eighties for which Gothic rock band?

9. With the exception of its subtitle '(Amazing)', the title of which number one for Bruno Mars could be mistaken as being a cover of an old Billy Joel song (*even though it isn't*!)?

10. Which of these two successful chart acts had the greater number of Top 10 singles during the seventies: Status Quo or Slade?

ANSWERS TO POPMASTER 10

1. 'Teenage Kicks' 2. Amy Winehouse 3. 'Pleasant Valley Sunday' 4. Julia Fordham 5. 'Blame It On Me' 6. Duffy 7. 'Teenage Dream' by Marc Bolan & T.Rex, 'Teenage Lament '74' by Alice Cooper 8. Nick Heyward 9. 'Island Of Dreams', 'Say I Won't Be There' (both peaked at No. 5 during 1963) 10. Orchestral Manoeuvres in the Dark

POPMASTER 12

1. In 1979, Squeeze had both a single and album called 'Cool For ____' what?

2. Who is the lead singer with Simple Minds?

3. Heaven 17 had two Top 10 hits in 1983. The first was 'Temptation'. What was the title of the second?

4. Who reached the Top 40 in 2005, 2012 and 2013 with his song 'Ordinary People'?

5. What '____ Hotel' did Chris Isaak sing about on his 1991 Top 20 single?

6 In 1975, the song 'It's In His Kiss' became the only Top 10 single for which singer?

7 American band Ohio Express made its only UK chart appearance in 1968 with which Top 5 song?

8 Which American family group made its only Top 40 appearance in 1987 with the Top 5 song 'Crush On You'?

9 The songs 'Skyscraper', 'Heart Attack' and 'Cool For The Summer' were all Top 10 hits in the 2010s for which singer?

10 What 1962 Top 10 song by The Everly Brothers was a Top 20 cover by a-ha in 1990?

ANSWERS TO POPMASTER 11

1. 'Rain On Me' 2. Jesus Jones 3. 'Woman In Love' 4. Georgie Fame 5. 'That's The Way (I Like It)' 6. Alisha's Attic 7. 'Hey Ya' (entered the chart in the Top 10, dipped down the chart before climbing back to its peak of No. 3 in 2004) 8. The Mission 9. 'Just The Way You Are (Amazing)' 10. Slade with 13, Status Quo had 9

POPMASTER 13

1. 'Panic' is the title of a 1986 Top 20 single by which group?

2. Girls Aloud confessed to having a lack of language skills on which 2008 Top 10 song?

3. The bands Pulp, The Human League, ABC and Moloko are just four of the chart acts to originate from which city in south Yorkshire?

4. Pink Floyd had two hit singles in the sixties. 'Arnold Layne' was one. What was the other called?

5. The songs 'Let The Music Play' and 'Give Me Tonight' were Top 40 singles in the first half of the eighties for which American singer?

6 Which song by James was Top 10 for the group in both 1991 and 1998?

7 Which popular singer in the sixties had a run of hits including 'Don't Sleep In The Subway', 'My Friend The Sea' and 'I Couldn't Live Without Your Love'?

8 Tinie Tempah featuring Tinashe had a Top 40 hit in 2017 with what '____ From Your Ex'?

9 'European Female' was a Top 10 single in the eighties for which group?

10 The New Seekers first reached the Top 40 in 1971 with the Top 3 single 'Never Ending ____' what?

ANSWERS TO POPMASTER 12

1. 'Cool For Cats' 2. Jim Kerr 3. 'Come Live With Me' 4. John Legend 5. 'Blue Hotel' 6. Linda Lewis 7. 'Yummy Yummy Yummy' 8. The Jets 9. Demi Lovato 10. 'Crying In The Rain'

POPMASTER 14

1. Richard Ashcroft of The Verve made his chart debut as a solo artist in 2000 with a Top 3 hit called 'A Song For ____' who or what?

2. Which duo sang 'Lovers Of The World Unite' on their 1966 Top 10 single?

3. In 1977, what two places in America are mentioned in the title of Patsy Gallant's Top 10 song?

4. The songs 'Your Game' in 2004, 'Switch It On' in 2005 and 'All Time Love' in 2006 were all Top 5 singles for which singer?

5. What 1989 single by De La Soul features samples of the Daryl Hall & John Oates song 'I Can't Go for That (No Can Do)'?

6 Who had a hit single in 2012 called 'I Knew You Were Trouble'?

7 What type of '____ Valley' did Love Affair sing about on the group's 1968 Top 5 song?

8 'It Ain't Over 'Til It's Over' was a Top 20 single in 1991 for which singer and guitarist?

9 In the changing line-up of Sugababes during their chart run from 2000 to 2010, what is the first name of the first member to leave the group?

10 The singer Jeffrey Osborne had his only two Top 40 hits in 1984. Both reached the Top 20. Can you name either of these?

ANSWERS TO POPMASTER 13

1. The Smiths 2. 'Can't Speak French' 3. Sheffield 4. 'See Emily Play' 5. Shannon 6. 'Sit Down' (Was originally released in 1989 but only reached No. 77; the 1998 hit is a remix of the original.) 7. Petula Clark 8. 'Text From Your Ex' 9. The Stranglers 10. 'Never Ending Song Of Love'

POPMASTER 15

1. Who is the lead singer with Garbage?

2. What 'Year _____' did Busted sing about on the group's 2003 Top 3 single?

3. Lee Graham had a Top 3 single in 1968 called 'Little Arrows'. Under what name did he record this song?

4. Beginning with the earliest, can you put these three songs by Diana Ross in the order they were originally hits for the singer: 'Upside Down', 'Surrender' and 'One Shining Moment'?

5. In 1977, who was 'Going In With My Eyes Open', according to the title of his Top 3 single?

6 Phil Manzanera had chart success throughout the seventies and early eighties as lead guitarist with which group?

7 What type of '_____ Dance' did Men Without Hats sing about in 1983, on their only Top 40 hit?

8 In 2023, 'Paint The Town Red' became the first UK number one for which American singer and rapper?

9 Meaning 'We Dance', what is the one-word title of the 1999 debut hit for Enrique Iglesias?

10 'I Can't Break Down' was a Top 3 song in 2003 for Sinead _____ who?

ANSWERS TO POPMASTER 14

1. 'A Song For The Lovers' 2. David & Jonathan 3. 'From New York To L.A.' 4. Will Young 5. 'Say No Go' 6. Taylor Swift 7. 'Rainbow Valley' 8. Lenny Kravitz 9. Siobhán (The original line-up reformed as Mutya, Keisha and Siobhán and in 2019 were once again known as Sugababes.) 10. 'Stay With Me Tonight' (No. 18), 'On The Wings of Love' (No. 11)

POPMASTER 16

1. In 1989, Debbie Gibson had both a Top 20 single and Top 10 album called 'Electric ____' what?

2. How many members are there in the South Korean boy band BTS?

3. Amen Corner reached number one in 1969 with '(If Paradise Is) Half As Nice', but three other singles in the sixties were Top 10 hits for the group. Can you name one of these?

4. What day of the week features in the title of a 1999 Top 20 single by David Bowie?

5. Which group made their chart debut in 1976 with the song 'Ships In The Night'?

6. Nena (1984), The Byrds (1966), Paul Simon (1976), Sam Fender (2021) and Vanessa Carlton (2002) have all had Top 40 singles with a numerical aspect to their titles. Can you work out the songs, then list the artists in ascending numerical order of their songs' titles?

7 The song 'Can't Be With You Tonight' spent a month at number 2 in 1987 for Judy ____ who?

8 Released in 2007, Shayne Ward's fourth and final Top 10 single has the same title as a number one for The Corrs in 2000. What is that shared title?

9 The group Racing Cars made their only Top 40 appearance in 1977 with which song?

10 Which band had the first of its five Top 40 hits in 1995 with 'Daydreamer' and had its only Top 10 single the following year with 'Being Brave'?

ANSWERS TO POPMASTER 15

1. Shirley Manson 2. 'Year 3000' 3. Leapy Lee 4. 'Surrender' (1971), 'Upside Down' (1980), 'One Shining Moment' (1992) 5. David Soul 6. Roxy Music 7. 'The Safety Dance' 8. Doja Cat 9. 'Bailamos' 10. Sinead Quinn

POPMASTER 17

1. Sonny & Cher reached number one in 1965 with which song?

2. A 1982 Top 5 single by Tight Fit and a 1997 Top 40 single by M People share the same two-word song title. What is that title?

3. The song 'Wish You The Best' entered the chart at number one in 2023 for which singer-songwriter?

4. What mode of transport features in the titles of hit songs in the seventies for both Queen and Nazareth and what are those titles?

5. 'Only One Road' was a Top 10 single in 1995 for which singer?

6 Released in 2021, the first single from Adele's album *30* spent a total of eight weeks at number one. What is it called?

7 'The Freeze' was a Top 20 single in 1981 for which group?

8 What did James Bay 'Hold Back _____' according to the title of his Top 3 song in the mid-2010s?

9 Which of these two successful chart acts had the greater number of Top 10 singles during the sixties: The Hollies or Herman's Hermits?

10 Two of Neil Diamond's hit singles in the seventies include the word 'Blue' in the title. 'Song Sung Blue' is one. What is the other?

ANSWERS TO POPMASTER 16

1. 'Electric Youth' 2. Seven (J-Hope, Jimin, Jin, Jungkook, RM, Suga,V) 3. 'Bend Me Shape Me' (No. 3 in 1968), 'High In The Sky' (No. 6 in 1968), 'Hello Suzie' (No. 4 in 1969) 4. Thursday - 'Thursday's Child' 5. Be Bop Deluxe 6. Byrds ('Eight Miles High'), Sam Fender ('Seventeen Going Under'), Paul Simon ('50 Ways To Leave Your Lover'), Nena ('99 Red Balloons'), Vanessa Carlton ('A Thousand Miles') 7. Judy Boucher 8. 'Breathless' 9. 'They Shoot Horses Don't They' 10. Menswear

POPMASTER 18

1. Who had a number one single in 2019 called 'Vossi Bop'?

2. Three of the Top 10 singles in the noughties for Natasha Bedingfield have one-word titles. Can you name one of these?

3. What links Daniel Bedingfield to Mika, Madness, Gorillaz and Haysi Fantayzee?

4. 'Angels With Dirty Faces' was the 1978 chart debut for which group?

5. Who had a Top 3 hit in 1966 with 'River Deep, Mountain High'?

6. The group Cock Robin made their only Top 40 appearance in 1986 with which song?

7 What is the title of Dario G's 1997 Top 3 debut, which contains a sample of 'Life In A Northern Town' by Dream Academy?

8 Who wanted to 'Let The Music Play' according to the title of his Top 10 hit in the mid-seventies?

9 The song 'About Damn Time' spent three months in the Top 10 in 2022 for which singer?

10 'Happy Together' was the first of three hits for The Turtles in the sixties, the other two reached the Top 10. Can you name either of these?

ANSWERS TO POPMASTER 17

1. 'I Got You Babe' 2. 'Fantasy Island' 3. Lewis Capaldi 4. Bicycle ('Bicycle Race' by Queen, 'My White Bicycle' by Nazareth) 5. Celine Dion 6. 'Easy On Me' (Entered at number one where it stayed for seven weeks, returned to No. 1 for a further week a little later.) 7. Spandau Ballet 8. 'Hold Back The River' 9. The Hollies (15 – they would have a further two in the 70s and a No. 1 in the 80s. Herman's Hermits – 9, and a further Top 10 hit at the start of the 70s.) 10. 'Forever In Blue Jeans'

POPMASTER 19

1. 'Mandinka' was the title of the 1988 Top 40 debut for which singer?

2. What 1979 Top 5 single for Dave Edmunds was written by Elvis Costello?

3. 'Let The Heartaches Begin' is the title of a 1967 number one for which artist?

4. In 2002, DJ Sammy and Yanou featuring Do had a big international hit with a dance version of which Bryan Adams song?

5. The song 'Stay (Faraway So Close)' was Top 5 in 1993 for which group?

6. Between 1952 and 2022 (70 years), the names of all seven colours of the rainbow feature in the title of at least one Top 10 single – except one! Which colour doesn't feature?

7. The album *Tin Drum* was released in 1981 and contained the hit singles 'Visions Of China', 'Ghosts' and 'Cantonese Boy'. Which group recorded it?

8. What type of '_____ Heart' did James Blunt sing about on his 2013 Top 5 song?

9. The writing and production team behind all of the hits in the seventies for Chic consisted of Nile Rodgers and who else?

10. Beyoncé and Shakira had a number one duet in 2007 with which song?

ANSWERS TO POPMASTER 18

1. Stormzy 2. 'Single' (2004 No. 3 chart debut), 'Unwritten' (No. 6 in 2004), 'Soulmate' (No. 7 in 2007) 3. They've all had hit singles with songs that have an actor's name in the title: 'James Dean (I Wanna Know)', 'Grace Kelly', 'Michael Caine', 'Clint Eastwood', 'John Wayne Is Big Leggy' 4. Sham 69 5. Ike & Tina Turner 6. 'The Promise You Made' 7. 'Sunchyme' 8. Barry White 9. Lizzo (a total of 13 weeks in the Top 10) 10. 'She'd Rather Be With Me' (No. 4 in '67), 'Elenore' (No. 7 in '68)

POPMASTER 20

1. 'Apollo 9' was a Top 20 single in 1984 for which singer?

2. What was Karen Ramirez 'Looking For ____' according to the title of her 1998 Top 10 single?

3. The songs 'Desire', 'Eyes Shut' and 'Shine' were all hits in the mid-2010s for which chart act?

4. With the official billing of 'Acker Bilk, his Clarinet and Strings', what was the title of his 1976 Top 5 instrumental – his only hit single in the seventies?

5. Which dance act followed up their 1992 number one 'Please Don't Go/Game Boy' with a Top 10 cover of the 1974 number one 'Rock Your Baby'?

6 The duo Marshall Hain had a Top 3 single in 1978 with which song?

7 Which group had a number one album in 2014 called *Education, Education, Education & War*?

8 Kyu Sakamoto had a Top 10 single and American number one in 1963 with which song?

9 What type of '_____ Day' did Haircut 100 sing about on the group's 1982 Top 10 single?

10 Who had a Top 5 instrumental hit in the late seventies called 'Song For Guy'?

ANSWERS TO POPMASTER 19

1. Sinead O'Connor 2. 'Girls Talk' 3. Long John Baldry 4. 'Heaven' 5. U2 6. Indigo (The highest charting single to feature that colour during the first 70 years of the chart was 'Indigo' by Moloko, which peaked at its chart entry of No. 51.) 7. Japan 8. 'Bonfire Heart' 9. Bernard Edwards (The first two hits 'Dance Dance Dance' and 'Everybody Dance' include a production credit for Kenny Lehman.) 10. 'Beautiful Liar'

POPMASTER 21

1 The songs 'Fell In Love With A Boy' and 'Super Duper Love (Are You Diggin On Me?)' were both Top 20 hits in 2004 for which singer?

2 Manfred Mann's Earth Band had a hit in 1973 with 'Joybringer', which was based on a piece of classical music. What is the piece and who composed it?

3 The songs 'How Sweet It Is (To Be Loved By You)', 'Road Runner' and 'What Does It Take (To Win Your Love)' were all hits in the sixties for which Tamla Motown act?

4 Katy Perry featured on a 2010 Top 3 song by Timbaland called 'If We Ever _____' what?

5 Who had a Top 5 double A-side at Christmas 1987 with 'My Arms Keep Missing You' and his version of the Nat 'King' Cole classic 'When I Fall In Love'?

6 Beginning with the earliest, put these three songs by The Who in the order they were originally hits: '5:15', 'I'm A Boy', You Better You Bet'?

7 The 1995 Top 10 song 'Chains' was the first UK chart appearance for which Australian singer?

8 How many '_____ Bicycles' are in Beijing according to Katie Melua's Top 5 song in 2005?

9 'Banana Splits (The Tra La La Song)' was a Top 10 single in 1979 for which group?

10 What is the one-word title of the 2021 Top 3 collaboration between Becky Hill and David Guetta?

ANSWERS TO POPMASTER 20

1. Adam Ant 2. 'Looking For Love' 3. Years & Years 4. 'Aria'
5. KWS 6. 'Dancing In The City' 7. Kaiser Chiefs 8. 'Sukiyaki'
(sold a reported 13 million copies worldwide) 9. 'Fantastic Day'
10. Elton John

POPMASTER 22

1. Complete the title of this 1998 number one by Manic Street Preachers: 'If You Tolerate This ____' what?

2. Who 'Wouldn't Change A Thing' according to the title of her 1989 Top 3 single?

3. The first two hits for Arctic Monkeys both reached number one. 'I Bet You Look Good On The Dancefloor' was the first in 2005. What was the second in 2006?

4. 'The Edge Of Glory' was a Top 10 song in 2011 for which singer?

5. What type of '____ Doll' did The Four Seasons sing about in 1964?

6 'There There My Dear', 'Show Me' and 'The Celtic Soul Brothers' were all singles in the early eighties for which group?

7 Who is the lead singer and guitarist with Stereophonics?

8 The titles of two of the hits for The Chi-Lites in the seventies end with the word 'Girl'. 'Homely Girl' is one. What is the other?

9 'Forever And For Always' was a Top 10 single in 2003. Who sang it?

10 In 1966, what day of the week did The Mama's and The Papa's sing about on their Top 3 single?

ANSWERS TO POPMASTER 21

1. Joss Stone 2. 'Jupiter, the Bringer of Jollity' from *The Planets* by Gustav Holst 3. Jr. Walker and the All Stars 4. 'If We Ever Meet Again' 5. Rick Astley 6. 'I'm A Boy' (1966), '5:15' (1973), 'You Better You Bet' (1981) 7. Tina Arena 8. 'Nine Million Bicycles' 9. The Dickies 10. 'Remember'

POPMASTER 23

1. What was '_____ On Your Collar' according to the title of Connie Francis' 1959 Top 3 hit?

2. The songs 'View From A Bridge' and 'Water On Glass' were hits in the early eighties for which singer?

3. What 2012 number one by Maroon 5 featured Wiz Khalifa?

4. Which member of the Spice Girls was 'Not Such An Innocent Girl' according to the title of her 2001 Top 10 solo single?

5. Originally released in 1996, Olive reached number one in 1997 with a remixed version of which song?

6 Can you name the American group that made their UK chart debut in 1976 with the song 'Rock 'N' Me'?

7 What is the one-word title of the song that spent ten weeks at number one in 2023 for Dave & Central Cee?

8 'Viva Bobby Joe' is the title of a 1969 Top 10 single by which group?

9 Sugar Minott had his only Top 40 single in 1981 with which Top 5 song?

10 Which Irish duo reached the Top 40 in 2011 with their Eurovision entry 'Lipstick'?

ANSWERS TO POPMASTER 22

1. 'If You Tolerate This Your Children Will Be Next' 2. Kylie Minogue 3. 'When The Sun Goes Down' 4. Lady Gaga 5. 'Rag Doll' 6. Dexy's Midnight Runners ('Show Me' & 'Celtic Soul Brothers' written as Dexys Midnight Runners) 7. Kelly Jones 8. 'Oh Girl' (No. 14 in 1972, also No. 5 in 1975 alongside 'Have You Seen Her?') 9. Shania Twain 10. 'Monday Monday' (The original labels of all their UK hits in the sixties include apostrophes in the group's name; their sixties singles that didn't reach the chart don't!)

POPMASTER 24

1 The singer Marilyn had a Top 5 hit in 1983 with which song?

2 The songs 'You're The Reason Why', 'Under One Roof' and 'Baby I Know' were the final three Top 40 singles in the seventies for which group?

3 In 2006, Beatfreakz had a Top 3 single with a dance version of which eighties hit?

4 Saffron is the name of the lead singer with the group that had Top 40 hits in 1997 with 'Ready To Go' and 'Drop Dead Gorgeous'. What is the name of the group?

5 What type of '_____ Reggae' featured in the title of Boris Gardiner's 1970 hit instrumental?

6 Which band had hit albums in the 2010s called *An Awesome Wave*, *This Is All Yours* and *Relaxer*?

7 Bert Weedon's 'Nashville ____' in 1959, Buzz Clifford's 'Baby Sittin' ____' in 1961, Hank C. Burnette's 'Spinning Rock ____' in 1976 and Little Benny and the Masters' 'Who Comes To ____' in 1985 are all missing the same word from their titles. What is that word?

8 Who commanded 'Shut Up And Drive' on her 2007 Top 5 single?

9 Camila Cabello featuring Ed Sheeran had a Top 10 hit in 2022 with which song?

10 'Move Any Mountain', 'Boss Drum' and 'Phorever People' were all Top 5 singles in the early nineties for which chart act?

ANSWERS TO POPMASTER 23

1. 'Lipstick On Your Collar' 2. Kim Wilde 3. 'Payphone' 4. Victoria Beckham 5. 'You're Not Alone' 6. Steve Miller Band 7. 'Sprinter' 8. The Equals 9. 'Good Thing Going (We've Got A Good Thing Going)' 10. Jedward

POPMASTER 25

1. Which of these two successful chart acts had the greater number of Top 10 singles during the nineties: Boyzone or East 17?

2. Despite having a run of critically acclaimed albums, Steely Dan only ever had two Top 40 singles, both of which came in the mid-seventies. Can you name either of these?

3. Written by lead singer Reg Presley, which group had a Top 5 hit in 1967 with 'Love Is All Around'?

4. Dua Lipa first reached number one in 2017 with which song?

5. Which group sang about 'The Second Summer Of Love' on their second and final Top 40 hit in the late eighties?

6 Martine McCutcheon had her fifth and final Top 40 single in 2001 with a Top 10 cover of which Donna Summer hit?

7 'Wrapping Paper', 'Strange Brew' and 'I Feel Free' were all hits in the sixties for which band?

8 What '_____Town' did UB40 sing about on the group's 1990 Top 5 single?

9 'Patience' is the title of a 2006 number one by Take That, but which singer had a number one album in 2004 with that same title?

10 Gloria Gaynor made her chart debut in the mid-seventies with which Top 3 song?

ANSWERS TO POPMASTER 24

1. 'Calling Your Name' 2. The Rubettes 3. 'Somebody's Watching Me' (was originally a hit for Rockwell with uncredited vocals by Michael Jackson) 4. Republica ('Ready To Go' originally released in 1996, but just missed the Top 40.) 5. 'Elizabethan Reggae' 6. Alt-J 7. 'Boogie' 8. Rihanna 9. 'Bam Bam' 10. The Shamen

POPMASTER 26

1. 'London Calling' is the title of both a 1979 single and album by which group?

2. The Divine Comedy made its chart debut in 1996 with which Top 20 single?

3. Who sang about 'My Future' on her 2020 Top 10 hit?

4. In the summer of 2000, both Melanie C and Christina Aguilera had hit singles with songs that shared the same title. What is that title?

5. The 1982 song 'Take A Chance With Me' was the last original hit for which group?

6 PP Arnold reached the Top 20 in 1967 with her debut hit. What was it called?

7 The 2018 number one 'Promises' is a collaboration between Calvin Harris and which singer?

8 Guy Darrell made his only chart appearance in 1973 with a song he'd recorded in the mid-sixties. What is the title of his Top 20 song?

9 Who reached the Top 10 in 1990 with his version of the Bee Gees song 'To Love Somebody'?

10 Which 2008 Top 5 single by will.i.am featured guest vocals by Cheryl Cole?

ANSWERS TO POPMASTER 25

1. Boyzone (16) (East 17 had 11, including 'If You Ever' with Gabrielle; or 12, including a single released as E-17 following the departure of Tony Mortimer.) 2. 'Do It Again', 'Haitian Divorce' 3. The Troggs 4. 'New Rules' 5. Danny Wilson 6. 'On The Radio' 7. Cream 8. 'Kingston Town' 9. George Michael 10. 'Never Can Say Goodbye'

POPMASTER 27

1. Who sang the theme song to the 1989 James Bond film *Licence To Kill*?

2. Only one of Donny Osmond's three number ones doesn't contain the word 'Love' somewhere in the title. What is it called?

3. 'Strangers' is the title of a 2018 Top 10 song by which Norwegian singer?

4. Farley 'Jackmaster' Funk had his only Top 40 hit of the eighties in 1986 with the song 'Love Can't _____' what?

5. Shaun Ryder had hits in the early nineties with 'Kinky Afro', 'Step On' and 'Loose Fit' as the lead singer with which group?

6 Leona Lewis reached number one in 2008 with her version of which Snow Patrol song?

7 Which American singer-songwriter had a debut hit in 1977 with 'Roadrunner'?

8 What type of '_____ Cat' did Janet Jackson sing about on her 1990 Top 20 single?

9 The band Vanilla Fudge made their only chart appearance in 1967 with their version of which Supremes hit?

10 Who declared 'We'll Bring The House Down' on their 1981 Top 10 single?

ANSWERS TO POPMASTER 26

1. The Clash 2. 'Something For The Weekend' 3. Billie Eilish 4. 'I Turn To You' 5. Roxy Music (The 1975 hit 'Love Is The Drug' returned to the Top 40 for one week in 1996.) 6. 'The First Cut Is The Deepest' 7. Sam Smith 8. 'I've Been Hurt' 9. Jimmy Somerville 10. 'Heartbreaker'

POPMASTER 28

1. Japan's David Sylvian had a Top 20 solo single in 1984 called 'Red ____' what?

2. 'The Music's No Good Without You' was a Top 10 song in 2001 for which singer?

3. Beginning with the earliest, put these three songs by The Rolling Stones in the order they were originally hits: 'Undercover Of The Night', 'Miss You', 'Not Fade Away'?

4. Which singer featured on Professor Green's 2011 number one 'Read All About It'?

5. In the mid-seventies, what type of '____ Weekend' did The Stylistics sing about on their Top 10 single?

6 Which group was billed alongside Billy J Kramer on the 1964 number one 'Little Children'?

7 What 1996 Top 10 single by Sleeper has the same title as a TV game show in the seventies hosted by Nicholas Parsons?

8 Who had a number one album in 2020 called *Music Played By Humans*?

9 The group It's Immaterial made their only Top 40 appearance in 1986, with a Top 20 song subtitled '(Jim's Tune)'. What is its full title?

10 Which German dance act wanted us to 'Evacuate The Dancefloor' on their 2009 number one?

ANSWERS TO POPMASTER 27

1. Gladys Knight 2. 'The Twelfth Of Never' 3. Sigrid 4. 'Love Can't Turn Around' (The song reached the Top 40 again in a re-recording with Darryl Pandy in 1996.) 5. Happy Mondays 6. 'Run' 7. Jonathan Richman 8. 'Black Cat' 9. 'You Keep Me Hanging On' (Group was officially billed as The Vanilla Fudge on the label.) 10. Slade

POPMASTER 29

1. In 2023, which song gave Kylie Minogue her first solo Top 10 hit in thirteen years?

2. Which group recorded the 1986 Top 20 hit 'And She Was'?

3. The Yardbirds made the Top 3 in 1965 with their double-A side hit, 'Evil Hearted You' and which other song?

4. According to their 1967 Top 10 hit, which group claimed: 'There's A Kind Of Hush'?

5. The subtitle '(But My Baby Loves To Dance)' belongs to a 1976 number one by Tina Charles. What is it actually called?

6 Which group sang about 'Virtual Insanity' in 1996?

7 The reggae singer and rapper Laza Morgan featured on which 2010 number one by Alexandra Burke?

8 'You Have Killed Me' was a 2006 Top 3 hit for which performer?

9 Sting first reached the Top 40 as a solo artist in 1982 with which Top 20 single?

10 Which female singer duetted with Marvin Gaye on the 1968 Top 20 hit 'You're All I Need To Get By'?

ANSWERS TO POPMASTER 28

1. 'Red Guitar' 2. Cher 3. 'Not Fade Away' (1964), 'Miss You' (1978), 'Undercover Of The Night' (1983) 4. Emeli Sandé 5. 'Funky Weekend' 6. Billy J Kramer & The Dakotas 7. 'Sale Of The Century' 8. Gary Barlow 9. 'Driving Away From Home (Jim's Tune)' 10. Cascada

POPMASTER 30

1. From 2022, who, in her Top 5 single, claimed to be a 'Super Freaky Girl'?

2. The first sales chart was published in November 1952, but what record was at number one?

3. The 1995 singles 'Yes' and 'You Do' and the 2002 songs 'Falling' and 'Bring It Back' were all Top 40 hits for McAlmont and _____ who?

4. Sally Oldfield, sister of Mike, had her only Top 40 hit in the late seventies with which Top 20 song?

5. The 1983 Top 20 single 'Christian' and the 1984 Top 10 song 'Wishful Thinking' were both hits for which Liverpudlian chart act?

6 In 2007, Shayne Ward made the Top 3 with his double A-side hit 'No U Hang Up' and which other song?

7 Who wrote and produced Nancy Sinatra's 1966 number one, 'These Boots Are Made For Walkin''?

8 The singer Babybird had his only Top 10 single in 1996. What was it called?

9 In 2020, 'Say So' was a Top 3 hit for which American rapper and singer?

10 The Climax Blues Band made their only Top 40 appearance in 1976 with which Top 10 song?

ANSWERS TO POPMASTER 29

1. 'Padam Padam' (Her first solo Top 10 since 'All The Lovers' in 2010, though in 2011 she featured as guest vocalist on Taio Cruz's Top 10 single 'Higher'.) 2. Talking Heads 3. 'Still I'm Sad' 4. Herman's Hermits 5. 'I Love To Love (But My Baby Loves To Dance)' 6. Jamiroquai 7. 'Start Without You' 8. Morrissey 9. 'Spread A Little Happiness' 10. Tammi Terrell

POPMASTER 31

1. What is the title of the 1975 number one by the American vocal group, The Tymes?

2. Can you name the group that had a Top 3 album in 2015 called *Anthems For Doomed Youth*?

3. Complete the title of this 1980 Top 3 single by Randy Crawford: 'One Day I'll _____' what?

4. Which instrument did Rick Wright play in Pink Floyd?

5. Released in 1962, what song became a Top 20 duet for Frank Sinatra and Sammy Davis Jr?

6 'I Gotta Feeling' and 'Meet Me Halfway' are titles of number ones in 2009 for which group?

7 *Woodface* was the 1991 breakthrough album by Crowded House. It contained four Top 40 singles. Can you name one of them?

8 'Cruel Summer' is the title of a 2023 Top 3 song for which singer?

9 Crispian St Peters reached the Top 5 on two occasions during the sixties, the first was with 'You Were On My Mind', but what was the title of the second?

10 By what name is English rapper Jahmaal Noel Fyffe better known?

ANSWERS TO POPMASTER 30

1. Nicki Minaj 2. 'Here In My Heart' by Al Martino 3. McAlmont & Butler 4. 'Mirrors' 5. China Crisis 6. 'If That's OK With You' 7. Lee Hazlewood 8. 'You're Gorgeous' 9. Doja Cat 10.'Couldn't Get It Right'

POPMASTER 32

1. The song 'When Smokey Sings' was a hit in 1987 for which group?

2. What four words in brackets complete the title of George Michael's 2004 Top 10 hit 'Flawless'?

3. 'What Now My Love?' was a Top 5 hit in 1962 for Shirley Bassey, but which duo took the song back into the Top 20 in 1966?

4. Jamaican band The Pioneers had their biggest UK hit in 1971 with which Top 5 song?

5. With which group do you associate Fran Healy, Dougie Payne, Andy Dunlop and Neil Primrose?

6. Complete the title of this 2013 Top 20 song by Eliza Doolittle: 'Big When I ____' what?

7 'My Doorbell' and 'The Denial Twist' were both Top 10 hits in 2005 for which successful act?

8 The Prodigy had both of their number one singles in 1996. 'Firestarter' was the first. What was the second?

9 What was the name of Sam the Sham's backing group that featured on the 1965 Top 20 hit 'Wooly Bully'?

10 On which 1975 single by T.Rex does Marc Bolan sing about a woman with a frog in her hand?

ANSWERS TO POPMASTER 31

1. 'Ms Grace' (Released in 1974, reached No. 1 in mid-January 1975.) 2. The Libertines 3. 'One Day I'll Fly Away' 4. Keyboards 5. 'Me And My Shadow' 6. Black Eyed Peas 7. 'Fall At Your Feet', 'Weather With You', 'Four Seasons In One Day', 'It's Only Natural' (the album's first single 'Chocolate Cake' only reached No. 69) 8. Taylor Swift (The song had charted for one week in 2019 when parent album Lover was released, but it became popular after its appearance in the set list of her 2023 'Eras Tour'.) 9. 'The Pied Piper' (No. 5 in 1966) 10. Chip (previously Chipmunk)

POPMASTER 33

1 In 2000, Mousse T featured on the Top 3 single 'Sex Bomb' by which legendary singer?

2 Frances Ruffelle represented the UK at Eurovision in 1994 with the song 'Lonely _____' what?

3 Released in 2016 and featuring Sean Paul and Anne-Marie, which chart act spent nine weeks at number one with the song 'Rockabye'?

4 Lonnie Donegan's 1960 Top 5 single, 'I Wanna Go Home', became a hit again in 1966 when it reached the Top 3 for The Beach Boys – but under a different title. What was it called?

5 Which singer made her Top 40 debut in 1989 with the Top 5 song 'Stop'?

6 The title of which Alvin Stardust single from 1974 is the same word repeated three times?

7 'Catch A Falling Star' is the title of a 1958 hit for which singer?

8 The Charlatans first reached the Top 40 in 1990 with which Top 10 song?

9 Who had a number one album called *There's Nothing But Space, Man!* in 2022?

10 Two of Gwen Stefani's Top 10 singles in 2005 have titles that end with the word 'Girl'. Can you name either of them?

ANSWERS TO POPMASTER 32

1. ABC 2. 'Flawless (Go To The City)' 3. Sonny & Cher (Their version omitted the '?' in the title.) 4. 'Let Your Yeah Be Yeah' 5. Travis 6. 'Big When I Was Little' 7. The White Stripes 8. 'Breathe' 9. The Pharaohs 10. 'New York City'

POPMASTER 34

1 'Pyramid Song' was a 2001 Top 5 single for which band?

2 Although different songs, what title provided Top 10 hits for Leroy Van Dyke in 1962 and Dionne Warwick in 1964?

3 Who was featured alongside Maroon 5 on the group's 2018 Top 10 song 'Girls Like You'?

4 'We Are Glass' was a 1980 Top 5 single for which artist?

5 In 1999, the American group Semisonic made their chart debut with the song 'Secret ____' what?

6 The songs 'Don't Stop', 'You Make Loving Fun' and 'Songbird' on Fleetwood Mac's *Rumours* were all written by which member of the group?

7 Released in 1968, Edwin Starr made the Top 20 early in 1969 with his double A-side consisting of two re-issues from 1966, 'Stop Her On Sight (SOS)' and which other song?

8 On their 2005 Top 10 hit, which group sang about a 'Black And White Town'?

9 Written and produced by Nile Rodgers and Bernard Edwards, Sheila & B. Devotion reached the charts in 1979 with which song?

10 Which member of Little Mix made her solo chart debut in 2023 with the Top 20 song 'Don't Say Love'?

ANSWERS TO POPMASTER 33

1. Tom Jones (taken from his No. 1 album *Reload*) 2. 'Lonely Symphony' 3. Clean Bandit 4. 'Sloop John B' 5. Sam Brown ('Stop' had originally been released in 1988, but failed to reach the Top 40.) 6. 'You You You' 7. Perry Como 8. 'The Only One I Know' 9. Sam Ryder 10. 'Rich Girl' (billed as Gwen Stefani featuring Eve), 'Hollaback Girl'

POPMASTER 35

1 Sugababes first reached number one in 2002 with a single that includes an interpolation of 'Are "Friends" Electric?' by Tubeway Army. What is it called?

2 'I Need A Dollar' was a Top 3 single in 2011 for which singer?

3 What two words in brackets begin the title of The Tremeloes' 1969 Top 3 hit '_____ Number One'?

4 Which group had Top 10 singles in 2004 with 'Matinée' and 'Take Me Out'?

5 What is the title of the 1979 Top 40 debut by The Pretenders? (And give yourself a pat on the back or a bonus point if you know who wrote it!)

6 Who had number ones in the fifties with the songs 'Such A Night', 'Just Walking In The Rain' and 'Yes Tonight Josephine'?

7 Which 1991 Top 10 single by Martika was co-written by the singer with Prince?

8 In 1981, which group confessed 'I'm In Love With A German Film Star'?

9 The band Foreigner first reached the Top 40 in 1978 with the song 'Feels Like _____' what?

10 Who sang about 'This Year's Love' on his 2001 Top 20 single?

ANSWERS TO POPMASTER 34

1. Radiohead 2. 'Walk On By' 3. Cardi B 4. Gary Numan 5. 'Secret Smile' 6. Christine McVie 7. 'Headline News' 8. Doves 9. 'Spacer' (Some pressings have the label credit as Sheila B Devotion.) 10. Leigh-Anne (Pinnock)

POPMASTER 36

1. In 1965, 'I Can't Explain' became the debut chart hit for which legendary group?

2. Which hit for The Boo Radleys has part of the band's name in its title?

3. The song 'I'm A Freak' reached the Top 5 in 2014 for Enrique Iglesias and which American rapper?

4. The biggest hit for French musician Cerrone came in 1978 with which Top 10 single?

5. Which vocal group reached number one in 2000 with the song 'Black Coffee'?

6. Singer-songwriter Tom Odell had two Top 10 singles in the 2010s. Both have titles that end with the word '_____ Love'. Can you name either of them?

7 Based on his Piano Concerto No. 1, which group had a Top 40 hit in 1966 called 'Tchaikovsky One'?

8 American band The Rainmakers made their only UK chart appearance in 1987 with which Top 20 song?

9 '(Turn Your Radio On)' is the subtitle to a 1992 Top 20 song by Shakespears Sister. What is its full title?

10 Dan Gillespie Sells is lead singer with the group whose hits in the noughties include 'Sewn', 'Love It When You Call' and 'I Thought It Was Over'. Can you name the group?

ANSWERS TO POPMASTER 35

1. 'Freak Like Me' 2. Aloe Blacc 3. '(Call Me) Number One' 4. Franz Ferdinand 5. 'Stop Your Sobbing' (Ray Davies) 6. Johnnie Ray 7. 'Love…Thy Will Be Done' 8. The Passions 9. 'Feels Like The First Time' 10. David Gray

POPMASTER 37

1 Yazz and the Plastic Population reached number one in 1988 with which single?

2 *Hypersonic Missiles* in 2019 and *Seventeen Going Under* in 2021 have both been number one albums for which singer-songwriter?

3 Beginning with the earliest, can you put these versions of the song 'Word Up' in the order they originally reached the charts: Little Mix, Cameo, Melanie B (as Melanie G), Gun?

4 Denise Marsa was the uncredited vocalist who sang alongside Dean Friedman on which 1978 Top 3 single?

5 The single 'Yoshimi Battles The Pink Robots Part 1' was Top 20 in 2003 for which American group?

6 In 1996, Warren G featuring Adina Howard reached the Top 3 with a single based on a Top 3 hit for Tina Turner in 1984, but featuring new lyrics. What is the song?

7 Can you name the pianist (with hits in his own right) who accompanied Dorothy Squires on the 1961 Top 40 song, 'Say It With Flowers'?

8 The final Top 10 hit for Bucks Fizz was a 1986 single subtitled '(Mamba Seyra)'. What is its full title?

9 Who had a number one in 2015 with the song 'Hold My Hand' and also featured on Tinie Tempah's number one 'Not Letting Go' that same year?

10 In 1966, The Mindbenders had a Top 3 hit with a song that would be a Top 40 solo single for Les Gray of Mud in 1977, and then number one in 1988 for Phil Collins. What is it called?

ANSWERS TO POPMASTER 36

1. The Who 2. 'Wake Up Boo!' 3. Pitbull 4. 'Supernature' 5. All Saints 6. 'Another Love' (No. 10 in 2013), 'Real Love' (No. 7 in 2014) 7. The Second City Sound 8. 'Let My People Go-Go' 9. 'Hello (Turn Your Radio On)' 10. The Feeling

POPMASTER 38

1 Which duo sang about 'Nobody's Diary' on their Top 3 single in 1983?

2 What was the title of the last number one single for The Rolling Stones during the sixties?

3 Who had a Top 10 cover of '7 Nation Army' in 2012, originally by The White Stripes?

4 In the seventies, drummer Cozy Powell had three hit singles. 'Dance With The Devil' was the first, can you name one of the other two?

5 The songs 'She's So Lovely', 'Elvis Ain't Dead' and 'Heartbeat' were Top 10 singles in the second half of the noughties for which group?

6 The songs 'Paradise' in 1988 and 'No Ordinary Love' in 1992 were the last Top 40 hit of the eighties and first of the nineties for which chart act?

7 In 2017, Liam Gallagher had his first solo Top 40 hit with the song 'Wall Of ____' what?

8 The songs 'Cruel Summer', 'Always Have, Always Will' and 'Everytime It Rains' were all hits in the late nineties for which group?

9 Which of the emergency services provided The Move with the title of their 1968 Top 3 single?

10 What did Missy Elliott 'Lose ____' according to the title of her Top 10 hit in 2005?

ANSWERS TO POPMASTER 37

1. 'The Only Way Is Up' 2. Sam Fender 3. Cameo (1986), Gun (1994), Melanie B (as Melanie G) (1999), Little Mix (2014) 4. 'Lucky Stars' 5. The Flaming Lips 6. 'What's Love Got To Do With It' 7. Russ Conway (Conway had eighteen Top 40 singles including two number ones.) 8. 'New Beginning (Mamba Seyra)' 9. Jess Glynne 10. 'Groovy Kind Of Love'

POPMASTER 39

1 'Imagine' was a posthumous number one in 1981 for which artist?

2 In 1984, Kool & The Gang had a Top 3 double A-side with 'Joanna' and which other song?

3 Prior to both his solo career and hits with Bernard Sumner as Electronic, Johnny Marr was guitarist with which Manchester band?

4 Mike McGear made his only Top 40 appearance in 1974 with which song?

5 The Real Thing, The Teardrop Explodes, The Icicle Works and The Christians were all formed in which city?

6 Having already had a couple of Top 40 hits, the Northern Ireland band Ash had their first Top 10 single in 1996 with a song that shares its title with a James Bond film. What is that title?

7 Which group of brothers had a Top 10 single in 2005 called 'Penny & Me'?

8 Olly Murs' chart career began in 2010 with which number one single?

9 In the mid-seventies, the song 'Are You Ready To Rock' became the final original Top 10 hit for which group?

10 In 1973, Eric Weissberg and Steve Mandell had a Top 20 instrumental called 'Dueling Banjos', a tune featured in the soundtrack to which film starring Jon Voigt and Burt Reynolds?

ANSWERS TO POPMASTER 38

1. Yazoo 2. 'Honky Tonk Women' 3. Marcus Collins (Collins' version was called 'Seven Nation Army') 4. 'The Man In Black', 'Na Na Na' 5. Scouting For Girls 6. Sade ('No Ordinary Love' was re-issued in 1993 and charted higher than its 1992 position.) 7. 'Wall Of Glass' 8. Ace Of Base 9. 'Fire Brigade' 10. 'Lose Control'

POPMASTER 40

1 Fleur East made her Top 40 debut in 2015 with which Top 3 song?

2 The song 'Swing Your Daddy' was Top 5 in 1975 for Jim _____ who?

3 The Righteous Brothers' recording of 'Unchained Melody' spent a month at number one in 1990 following its use in the pottery scene of which feature film?

4 Which singer made his feature film debut in Christopher Nolan's *Dunkirk*?

5 Despite nine Top 40 hits, only one of All About Eve's singles reached the Top 10. Released in 1988, what was it called?

6 In 1976, the song 'Shannon' became the only UK hit for American singer-songwriter Henry _____ who?

7 Which song has been number one in 1959 for Bobby Darin, a Top 20 hit for Ella Fitzgerald in 1960, but had its title relegated to a subtitle for Louis Armstrong's recording of 'A Theme from The Threepenny Opera' in 1956?

8 What is the only song written by George Harrison on the Beatles album *Sgt Pepper's Lonely Hearts Club Band*?

9 Which punk-era band had their biggest hit in 1986 with a cover of the Barry Ryan hit 'Eloise'?

10 Released in 2017, Eminem featuring Ed Sheeran reached number one early the following year with which song?

ANSWERS TO POPMASTER 39

1. John Lennon 2. 'Tonight' 3. The Smiths 4. 'Leave It' 5. Liverpool 6. 'Goldfinger' 7. Hanson 8. 'Please Don't Let Me Go' 9. Wizzard (The seasonal hit 'I Wish It Could Be Christmas Everyday' has returned to the Top 10 since then.) 10. *Deliverance*

PICK 'N' MIX

Right, now you're all sitting comfortably, let's mix things up a bit! Coming up in this section, we've thirty sets of themed questions. All the decades are covered in a variety of subjects – some of which will be a little trickier than others.

ONE FOR THE ALBUM

Below are the first and last tracks of UK number one albums along with the year the album reached number one (which might not be the year of release). Can you name the album and who recorded it? Tracks are from the standard original release, not deluxe or expanded editions, and are certified platinum or multi-platinum albums.

1. 'Eagle' and 'I'm A Marionette' - 1978
2. 'Politik' and 'Amsterdam' - 2002
3. 'Taxman' and 'Tomorrow Never Knows' - 1966
4. 'Cluster One' and 'High Hopes' - 1994
5. 'Spirits In The Material World' and 'Darkness' - 1981

6 'Hello' and 'Sweetest Devotion' – 2015

7 'If You All Get To Heaven' and 'Who's Loving You' – 1987

8 'Hanging On The Telephone' and 'Just Go Away' – 1979

9 'Something Got Me Started' and 'Wonderland' – 1991

10 'High' and 'No Bravery' – 2005

ANSWERS TO POPMASTER 40

1. 'Sax' 2. Jim Gilstrap 3. *Ghost* 4. Harry Styles 5. 'Martha's Harbour' 6. Henry Gross 7. 'Mack The Knife' 8. 'Within You Without You' 9. The Damned (the group's only Top 10 single) 10. 'River'

'... AND ON DRUMS'

Can you name the well-known guests who played (or sang) on these hit singles?

1. 'Someday' by The Gap Band (harmonica)?

2. 'Love Train' by Holly Johnson (guitar)?

3. 'Leave A Light On' by Belinda Carlisle (slide guitar)?

4. 'No Regrets' by Robbie Williams (two backing vocalists, both with the same first name)?

5. 'Try' by Bros (bass guitar)?

6 'Left Of Center' by Suzanne Vega (piano)?

7 'No One Is To Blame' by Howard Jones (drums)?

8 'Oh Patti (Don't Feel Sorry For Loverboy)' by Scritti Politti (trumpet)?

9 'The Bitch Is Back' by Elton John (backing vocals)?

10 'You Should Be Dancing' by The Bee Gees (additional percussion)?

ANSWERS TO ONE FOR THE ALBUM

1. *ABBA: The Album*, ABBA (originally released in Scandinavia in 1977) 2. *A Rush Of Blood To The Head*, Coldplay 3. *Revolver*, The Beatles 4. *The Division Bell*, Pink Floyd 5. *Ghost In The Machine*, The Police 6. *25*, Adele 7. *Introducing The Hardline According To Terence Trent D'Arby*, Terence Trent D'Arby (entered chart at No. 1 in 1987, but would spend eight consecutive weeks at No. 1 in 1988) 8. *Parallel Lines*, Blondie (originally released in 1978.) 9. *Stars*, Simply Red 10. *Back To Bedlam*, James Blunt (originally released in 2004)

MISSING WORDS

What is the missing word that completes these Top 40 song titles?

1. '_____ Me' by Lewis Capaldi

2. 'Silver _____ Machine' by David Essex

3. 'Something's _____' by Kenny Rogers and The First Edition

4. 'One _____ Man' by Missy Elliott featuring Ludacris

5. 'Mr _____ (Man, It Was Mean)' by Steve Harley & Cockney Rebel

6 'Wide ____' by Nik Kershaw

7 'Just Give Me A ____' by P!nk featuring Nate Ruess

8 '____ Hour' by Sparks

9 'Here Comes That ____' by Brenda Lee

10 '____ (Bird Of Prey)' by Fatboy Slim

ANSWERS TO '... AND ON DRUMS'

1. Stevie Wonder 2. Brian May 3. George Harrison 4. Neil Tennant (Pet Shop Boys), Neil Hannon (Divine Comedy) 5. Mark King (Level 42) 6. Joe Jackson 7. Phil Collins (Collins also co-produced the single with Hugh Padgham) 8. Miles Davis 9. Dusty Springfield (along with Clydie King, Sherlie Matthews & Jessie Mae Smith) 10. Stephen Stills (Crosby, Stills & Nash)

MAGIC MOMENTS

Relive those 'Hot Diggity (Dog Ziggity Boom)' days of the 1950s!

1. What was the title of the first UK number one achieved by Elvis Presley?

2. In 1953, Danny Kaye made the Top 10 with his only hit single. What was the title?

3. In 1957 two versions of 'The Banana Boat Song' reached the Top 10. One was by Harry Belafonte, but who recorded the other?

4. Can you name the singer who spent five weeks at number one in the late fifties with 'It's Only Make Believe'?

5. Russ Conway topped the charts on two occasions in 1959, the first time was with 'Side Saddle', but what was the title of the second?

6 'High Class Baby' and 'Mean Streak' were both Top 10 singles for which legendary performer?

7 According to his 1952 Top 10 hit, who was 'Walkin' To Missouri'?

8 'Come Softly To Me' was a 1959 Top 10 song for The Kaye Sisters alongside which male vocalist?

9 On her 1956 Top 3 hit, who claimed to be a 'Sweet Old-Fashioned Girl'?

10 In November 1953, which singer held four of the Top 10 chart positions with his hits 'Answer Me', 'Hey Joe', 'I Believe' and 'Where The Winds Blow'?

ANSWERS TO MISSING WORDS

1. 'Forget Me' 2. 'Silver DREAM Machine' 3. 'Something's BURNING' 4. 'One MINUTE Man' 5. 'Mr RAFFLES (Man, It Was Mean)' 6. 'Wide BOY' 7. 'Just Give Me A REASON' 8. 'AMATEUR Hour' 9. 'Here Comes That FEELING' 10. 'SUNSET (Bird Of Prey)'

ANAGRAMS

Can you work out the titles of these hits in anagram form. But beware, the number of anagram words may not be the same as the number of words in the song title!

1 'Purveying No Go Avenue' by Rick Astley

2 'Meteor Hips' by Girls Aloud

3 'File Names Oven Hot Pot' by The Supremes

4 'Given Them Eight' by George Benson

5 'Tight Slop' by Jennifer Hudson

6 'Conveying Harmed Smog' by The Style Council

7 'Regulations Do Nag' by The Average White Band *(answer includes one apostrophe)*

8 'A Weaken Lawyer' by The Four Tops

9 'Banked Thigh Cloth' by The Trammps

10 'Thinking Legal Tat' by Harry Styles

ANSWERS TO MAGIC MOMENTS

1. 'All Shook Up' (No. 1 for seven weeks in 1957) 2. 'Wonderful Copenhagen' 3. Shirley Bassey (A third version by The Tarriers stalled at No. 15.) 4. Conway Twitty 5. 'Roulette' 6. Cliff Richard (both singles credit The Drifters alongside Cliff Richard) 7. Tony Brent 8. Frankie Vaughan 9. Teresa Brewer 10. Frankie Laine

MY LIFE STORY

Can you work out who these singers are from these brief biographies?

1. I was born in Memphis, Tennessee in 1981, was a member of the Mickey Mouse Club before becoming a member of a boy band. I launched my solo career in 2002 with the single 'Like I Love You' and my film roles include the voices of Arthur 'Artie' Pendragon in *Shrek The Third*, Boo Boo in *Yogi Bear* and Branch in *Trolls*.

2. I was born in Brooklyn, New York in the 1940s. I used to play piano for Bette Midler. My 1975 debut hit made number one for Westlife in 2003. One of my songs reached the Top 5 for Take That in 1992, but the only Top 10 single I've had myself was with the 1982 release 'I Wanna Do It With You'.

3 I was born Louisa Bobb in Hackney, London but use just my middle name when I record. I was voted Best British Newcomer at the 1994 Brit Awards, having had a number one with my debut chart single 'Dreams' the previous year. Other hits include a Top 10 duet with East 17 and a cover version of 'Walk On By'.

4 I was born in Ontario in 1959. I've had hit duets during my career with Tina Turner, Barbra Streisand and Melanie C and apart from a solo number one in 1991, I was guest vocalist on a number one in 2000 for Chicane called 'Don't Give Up'.

5 I was born in 1940 and died in 1983. I had 26 Top 40 hits between 1959 and 1966, including 'Halfway To Paradise', 'It's Only Make Believe' and 'I'd Never Find Another You'. A statue of me overlooks the Albert Dock in Liverpool.

CONTINUES OVERLEAF

6 I was born in Essex in 1991. As a child I auditioned for the musical *Les Misérables* and also appeared in *Whistle Down The Wind*. I'm a black belt of Shotokan Karate. I released my debut album *Speak Your Mind* in 2018 and had a Top 10 duet with James Arthur called 'Rewrite The Stars' that same year.

7 I was born in New York in 1951. I was a backing vocalist on David Bowie's 'Young Americans' and lead vocalist on 'The Glow of Love' by Change. I had my first Top 40 solo hit in 1987 with 'I Really Didn't Mean It' and 'Endless Love' with Mariah Carey reached the Top 3 in 1994.

8 I was born in the Bronx. I had my first UK hit in 1999 with 'If You Had My Love'. My 2011 number one 'On The Floor' featured Pitbull. I've been a judge on *American Idol*. I've also starred in several films including *Maid in Manhattan*, *Monster-in-Law* and *Second Act*.

9 I was born in New York in 1964. I made the Top 40 for the first time in 1990 with 'Let Love Rule' (also the title track of my first album), I co-wrote and produced Madonna's 'Justify My Love' and Vanessa Paradis' 'Be My Baby' and had a number one album in 1993 with *Are You Gonna Go My Way*.

10 I was born in Berkshire in 1979, my debut single in 2002 sold a reported 1.1 million copies in its first week. My debut album *From Now On* went to number one that same year. I appeared in the fourteenth series of *Strictly Come Dancing* and in 2006 had a hit single called 'Who Am I'.

ANSWERS TO ANAGRAMS

1. 'Never Gonna Give You Up' 2. 'The Promise' 3. 'Stop In The Name Of Love' 4. 'Give Me The Night' 5. 'Spotlight' 6. 'My Ever Changing Moods' 7. 'Let's Go Round Again' 8. 'Walk Away Renee' 9. 'Hold Back The Night' 10. 'Late Night Talking'

FIND THE HIT

Below are five songs by chart acts in the order they reached the Top 10, but which one is missing? (Beware, they might have had some lower charting hits in between!)

1. Craig David: '7 Days', 'Walking Away', _____, 'What's Your Flava', 'Hidden Agenda'
2. Madonna: 'Like A Prayer', 'Express Yourself', 'Cherish', 'Dear Jessie', _____
3. Mud: 'The Cat Crept In', _____, 'Lonely This Christmas', 'The Secrets That You Keep', 'Oh Boy'
4. U2: 'Hold Me, Thrill Me, Kiss Me, Kill Me', 'Discotheque', 'Staring At The Sun', _____, 'Please'
5. Bill Haley & His Comets: 'Rock Around The Clock', 'Rock-A-Beatin' Boogie', 'See You Later Alligator', 'The Saints Rock 'N Roll', _____

6 Ed Sheeran: 'Afterglow', 'Bad Habits', 'Visiting Hours', _____, 'Overpass Graffiti'

7 Manfred Mann: 'Do Wah Diddy Diddy', 'Sha La La', 'Come Tomorrow', 'If You Gotta Go, Go Now', _____

8 Jason Donovan: 'Too Many Broken Hearts', 'Sealed With A Kiss', _____, 'When You Come Back To Me', 'Hang On To Your Love'

9 Bobby Vee: 'Rubber Ball', 'More Than I Can Say', 'How Many Tears', _____, 'Run To Him'

10 Westlife: 'My Love', 'What Makes A Man', _____, 'Queen Of My Heart', 'World Of Our Own'

ANSWERS TO MY LIFE STORY

1. Justin Timberlake 2. Barry Manilow 3. Gabrielle 4. Bryan Adams 5. Billy Fury 6. Anne-Marie 7. Luther Vandross 8. Jennifer Lopez 9. Lenny Kravitz 10. Will Young

STUCK ON TWO

All these songs reached number two in the charts, but can you remember the song and chart act that stopped them reaching pole position?

1. 'Can't Stand Me Now' by The Libertines

2. 'One More Time' by Daft Punk

3. 'Get Sexy' by Sugababes

4. 'Put Your Records On' by Corinne Bailey-Rae

5. 'By The Way' by Red Hot Chili Peppers

6 'Perfect 10' by The Beautiful South

7 'Don't Know Much' by Linda Ronstadt featuring Aaron Neville

8 'When Forever Has Gone' by Demis Roussos

9 'Torn' by Natalie Imbruglia

10 'All Day And All Of The Night' by The Kinks

ANSWERS TO FIND THE HIT

1. 'Rendezvous' 2. 'Vogue' 3. 'Rocket' 4. 'Last Night On Earth' 5. 'Rockin' Through The Rye' (The single 'Mambo Rock' peaked at No. 14 between 'Rock Around The Clock' and 'Rock-A-Beatin' Boogie'.) 6. 'Shivers' 7. 'Pretty Flamingo' (The single 'Oh No Not My Baby' peaked at No. 11 between 'Come Tomorrow' and 'If You Gotta Go, Go Now'.) 8. 'Every Day (I Love You More)' 9. 'Take Good Care Of My Baby' 10. 'Uptown Girl'

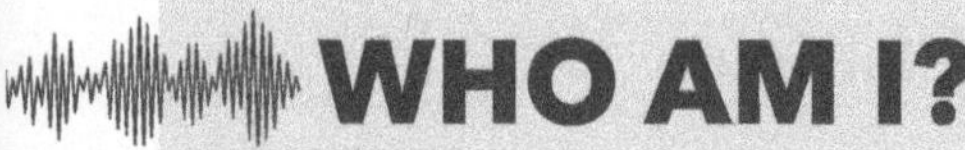

WHO AM I?

The first letter of each answer to the questions below spells out the name of which chart act?

1. Name the act whose only Top 10 hit was in 1988 with 'The Jack That House Built'?

2. 'Girl From Mars', 'Angel Interceptor', 'Oh Yeah' and 'A Life Less Ordinary' were all Top 20 hits in the nineties for which group?

3. What was the one-word title of the 1974 debut hit for Pilot?

4. From 1988, which group achieved their only Top 10 hit with the song 'Need You Tonight'?

5. What was the title of the 1986 debut hit and number one for Austrian singer Falco?

6 In 1984, Bob Marley and the Wailers made the Top 5 with a medley of two songs. One was 'People Get Ready', but what was the other?

7 Featuring guest vocals by Dina Carroll, 'It's Too Late' was a 1991 Top 10 single for which chart act?

8 Reaching the Top 10 in 1990, can you name the group that duetted with Robert Palmer on the song 'I'll Be Your Baby Tonight'?

9 Who wrote the musical *Evita* with Tim Rice?

10 What was the title of the first single by The Nolans to make the Top 10?

ANSWERS TO STUCK ON TWO

1. 'Babycakes' by 3 Of A Kind 2. 'Can't Fight The Moonlight' by Leann Rimes 3. 'Run This Town' by Jay-Z, Rihanna & Kanye West 4. 'Sorry' by Madonna 5. 'A Little Less Conversation' by Elvis vs JXL 6. 'Rollercoaster' by B*Witched 7. 'You Got It (The Right Stuff)' by New Kids on the Block 8. 'Mississippi' by Pussycat 9. 'Barbie Girl' by Aqua 10. 'Baby Love' by The Supremes

ALL AROUND THE WORLD

Each trio of Top 40 artists were either born or their groups were formed in the same country – but which country?

1. 'Substitute' by Clout (1978), 'Tokoloshe Man' by John Kongos (1971) and 'Lies' by Jonathan Butler (1987)?

2. 'Tilted' by Christine and the Queens (2016), 'Magic Fly' by Space (1977), 'Voyage Voyage' by Desireless (1988)?

3. 'Ride On Time' by Black Box (1989), 'Dolce Vita' by Ryan Paris (1983), 'Boys (Summertime Love)' by Sabrina (1988)?

4. 'Cupid' by Fifty Fifty (2023), 'How You Like That' by Blackpink (2020), 'Gangnam Style' by Psy (2012)?

5. 'Seven Tears' by Goombay Dance Band (1982), 'Axel F' by Harold Faltermeyer (1985), 'Wind Of Change' by Scorpions (1991)?

6 'Stitches' by Shawn Mendes (2015), 'Echo Beach' by Martha and the Muffins (1980), 'One Week' by Barenaked Ladies (1999)?

7 'Crying At The Discoteque' by Alcazar (2001), 'Y Viva Espana' by Sylvia (1974), 'Call On Me' by Eric Prydz (2004)?

8 'Venus' by Shocking Blue (1970), 'Up And Down' by Vengaboys (1998), 'You' by Ten Sharp (1992)?

9 'How Bizarre' by OMC (1996), 'Royals' by Lorde (2013), 'I Got You' by Split Enz (1980)?

10 'She Bangs' by Ricky Martin (2000), 'Light My Fire' by José Feliciano (1968), 'Gasolina' by Daddy Yankee (2005)?

ANSWERS TO WHO AM I?

1. Jack 'N' Chill (had previously been released in 1987, but didn't make the Top 40) 2. Ash 3. 'Magic' 4. INXS (originally released in 1987, but failed to make Top 40) 5. 'Rock Me Amadeus' 6. 'One Love' 7. Quartz (officially billed as 'Quartz introducing Dina Carroll') 8. UB40 9. Andrew Lloyd-Webber 10. 'I'm In The Mood For Dancing' Chart Act: Jamiroquai

ONE THING LEADS TO ANOTHER

Each question or answer has a link to the following question (so no looking ahead!).

1. Can you name the rapper who topped the charts in 2000 with 'Stan'?

2. Which Top 3 song by Dido was sampled on that Eminem hit?

3. 'Thank You' was included on the soundtrack to which 1998 movie that starred Gwyneth Paltrow and John Hannah?

4. Which singer-songwriter made the Top 40 in 1977 with 'Slip Slidin' Away'?

5. The Bangles made the Top 20 in 1988 with which Paul Simon composition?

6. The Edgar Winter Group reached the Top 40 in 1973 with which Top 20 instrumental?

7 In 1992, the film *Wayne's World* gave both Alice Cooper a Top 40 single with 'Feed My Frankenstein' and Tia Carrere a Top 40 cover version of which song?

8 What was the first Top 40 hit by The Sweet to be written by the band rather than the songwriting duo Nicky Chinn and Mike Chapman?

9 In 1987, Samantha Fox had a hit with a song subtitled '(To The Spirit Of The Night)'. What is its full title?

10 What is the name of the band formed by Ritchie Blackmore that had Top 10 hits with 'Since You've Been Gone', 'All Night Long' and 'I Surrender'?

ANSWERS TO ALL AROUND THE WORLD

1. South Africa 2. France ('Voyage Voyage' had originally been released in 1987, but only reached the Top 40 in 1988.) 3. Italy (Ryan Paris born Fabio Roscioli in Rome) 4. South Korea 5. Germany 6. Canada 7. Sweden 8. Netherlands 9. New Zealand 10. Puerto Rico

BESIDE THE B-SIDE

Celebrating the glory days of the seven-inch single. What number one was on the other side of these songs? Match the B-side with the A-side on the original seven-inch single and name the act. Give yourself a bonus point if you know the year it reached number one.

B-SIDE

1 'One February Friday'
2 'The Women'
3 'Mean Woman Blues'
4 'Woodpigeon Song'
5 'Baby Be Mine'
6 '(I'm Not Your) Steppin Stone'
7 'Don't Blame Me'
8 'The Fame'
9 'Good Times, Bad Times'
10 'All At Once'

A-SIDE

1 'I'm A Believer'
2 'It's All Over Now'
3 'Y.M.C.A.'

4 'Two Tribes'
5 'Great Balls Of Fire'
6 'Beetlebum'
7 'Saving All My Love For You'
8 'All Around The World'
9 'I Just Can't Stop Loving You'
10 'Merry Xmas Everybody'

CHART ACT

1 Slade
2 The Monkees
3 Whitney Houston
4 Village People
5 Blur
6 Frankie Goes To Hollywood
7 The Rolling Stones
8 Oasis
9 Jerry Lee Lewis
10 Michael Jackson with Siedah Garrett

ANSWERS TO ONE THING LEADS TO ANOTHER

1. Eminem 2. 'Thank You' 3. *Sliding Doors* 4. Paul Simon 5. 'A Hazy Shade Of Winter' 6. 'Frankenstein' 7. 'Ballroom Blitz' 8. 'Fox On The Run' 9. 'I Surrender (To The Spirit Of The Night)' 10. Rainbow

LUCKY NUMBER

There is only one perfect combination. Match a number with a chart act and give the title of the Top 40 song that contains that number.

Each number can be used only once and the word or number is as it appears in the song title.

NUMBERS

1 One
2 Two
3 Three
4 Four
5 5
6 6
7 7
8 8
9 9
10 Ten

CHART ACT

1 Mark Owen
2 The Stone Roses
3 The Associates
4 Ellie Goulding
5 Barry Biggs
6 Haircut 100
7 Lukas Graham
8 Sneaker Pimps
9 McFly
10 John Lennon

ANSWERS TO BESIDE THE B-SIDE

1. 'One February Friday' / 'Two Tribes' by Frankie Goes To Hollywood (1984) 2. 'The Women' / 'Y.M.C.A.' by Village People (1979) 3. 'Mean Woman Blues' / 'Great Balls Of Fire' by Jerry Lee Lewis (1958) 4. 'Woodpigeon Song' / 'Beetlebum' by Blur (1997) 5. 'Baby Be Mine' / 'I Just Can't Stop Loving You' by Michael Jackson with Siedah Garrett (1987) 6. '(I'm Not Your) Steppin Stone' / 'I'm A Believer' by The Monkees (1967) 7. 'Don't Blame Me' / 'Merry Xmas Everybody' by Slade (1973) 8. 'The Fame' / 'All Around The World' by Oasis (1998) 9. 'Good Times, Bad Times' / 'It's All Over Now' by The Rolling Stones (1964) 10. 'All At Once' / 'Saving All My Love For You' by Whitney Houston (1985)

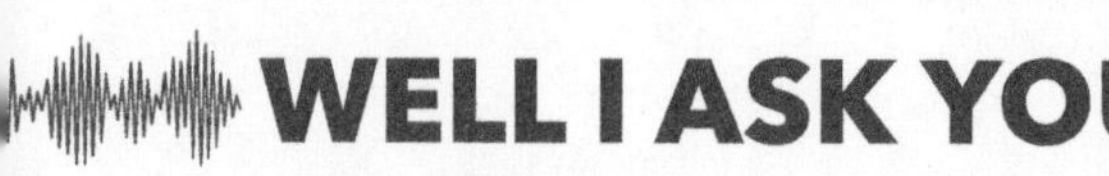

WELL I ASK YOU

Fingers crossed it's just Heinz Burt who has 'Questions I Can't Answer' from the 1960s!

1. 'Love Me Tender' and 'Hi-Lili, Hi-Lo' were both Top 20 hits in the first half of the sixties for which singing actor?

2. How many number one hits were achieved by Ray Charles during the sixties?

3. What was the name of the group that made the Top 20 in 1969 with an instrumental version of *'Je T'Aime _____ Moi Non Plus'* under the title 'Love At First Sight'?

4. 'But You're Mine' and 'Little Man' were both Top 20 hits in the mid-sixties for which husband and wife act?

5. Which Lennon and McCartney song was a Top 10 hit for The Young Idea in 1967 and a number one for Joe Cocker a year later?

6 According to his only hit, who in 1963 was 'Swinging On A Star'?

7 'I'm A Better Man' and 'Winter World Of Love' were the last two Top 20 hits of the sixties for which successful singer?

8 *'Si Tu Dois Partir'* was a 1969 Top 40 hit for Fairport Convention. It was a French language version of which Bob Dylan song?

9 '1-2-3' was the first of two Top 10 hits for Len Barry. What was the title of the other?

10 Can you name the musical from which Bobbie Gentry's 1969 number one 'I'll Never Fall In Love Again' was taken?

ANSWERS TO LUCKY NUMBER

1. 'Love Plus One' by Haircut 100 (1982) 2. 'Party Fears Two' by The Associates (1982) 3. 'Three Ring Circus' by Barry Biggs (1977) 4. 'Four Minute Warning' by Mark Owen (2003) 5. '5 Colours In Her Hair' by McFly (2004) 6. '6 Underground' by Sneaker Pimps (1996) (A 1997 remixed version was written as 'Six'.) 7. '7 Years' by Lukas Graham (2016) 8. 'Figure 8' by Ellie Goulding (2012) 9. '# 9 Dream' by John Lennon (1975) 10. 'Ten Storey Love Song' by The Stone Roses (1995)

ANAGRAMS

Can you work out the titles of these hits in anagram form? As before, the number of anagram words may not be the same as the number of words in the song title!

1. 'Contrastingly Be The Gent' by D:Ream
2. 'Horsewomen Won Weekly' by Keane
3. 'Heaven Hefted Ego' by Wham
4. 'Boneless Doctor' by Paloma Faith
5. 'Dismiss Wrong' by The Selecter

6 'Chevy Arms Resized' by Fine Young Cannibals

7 'Cooler Apiary Dummies' by Simple Minds

8 'My Westerly Title Set' by Wet Wet Wet

9 'Idling Telephoner' by Adele

10 'Say Elusively Afoot' by Matt Monro

ANSWERS TO WELL I ASK YOU

1. Richard Chamberlain 2. One ('I Can't Stop Loving You' in 1962) 3. Sounds Nice (full credit 'Sounds Nice featuring Tim Mycroft on organ') 4. Sonny & Cher 5. 'With A Little Help From My Friends' 6. Big Dee Irwin 7. Engelbert Humperdinck 8. 'If You Gotta Go, Go Now' 9. 'Like A Baby' 10. *Promises, Promises*

SAME SONG, DIFFERENT ACT

Here are the names of two chart acts who have both had hits with the same song. What is that title?

1. Smokey Robinson & The Miracles and The Beat

2. Peggy Lee and Helen Shapiro

3. The Four Seasons and Darts

4. Bill Haley & His Comets and Telex

5. David Bowie and The Merseys

6 Aswad and Ace Of Base

7 Richard Harris and Donna Summer

8 Mud and Club Nouveau

9 The Supremes and Bananarama

10 Tab Hunter and Donny Osmond

ANSWERS TO ANAGRAMS

1. 'Things Can Only Get Better' 2. 'Somewhere Only We Know' 3. 'The Edge Of Heaven' 4. 'Stone Cold Sober' 5. 'Missing Words' 6. 'She Drives Me Crazy' 7. 'Promised You A Miracle' 8. 'Sweet Little Mystery' 9. 'Rolling In The Deep' 10. 'Softly As I Leave You'

ONE THING LEADS TO ANOTHER

Each question or answer has a link to the following question (so no looking ahead!).

1. Which female singer duetted with Elton John on their 2022 Top 3 hit 'Hold Me Closer'?
2. What was the title of Britney Spears' first UK hit and number one?
3. The video of '... Baby One More Time' depicted Britney dancing in what type of uniform?
4. Who had a Top 20 hit in 1974 with 'School Love'?
5. In 1982, Barry co-wrote and produced the Top 10 hit 'I Eat Cannibals' for which female group?

6 Which group had a number one album in 1979 called *Eat To The Beat*?

7 Which number one hit by Blondie was covered by Atomic Kitten in 2002 to reach number one again?

8 Can you name the singer who achieved his first solo hit in 1966 with 'High Time'?

9 Featured in the movie *Lock, Stock And Two Smoking Barrels*, which group made the Top 5 in 1997 with 'Hundred Mile High City'?

10 Which football team had a Top 5 single in 1972 with 'Blue Is The Colour?

ANSWERS TO SAME SONG, DIFFERENT ACT

1. 'Tears Of A Clown' 2. 'Fever' (Helen Shapiro's final appearance in the singles chart) 3. 'Let's Hang On' 4. 'Rock Around The Clock' 5. 'Sorrow' 6. 'Don't Turn Around' 7. 'MacArthur Park' 8. 'Lean On Me' 9. 'Nathan Jones' 10. 'Young Love'

WHO AM I?

The first letter of each answer to the questions below spells out the name of which chart act?

1. 'Walk This Way' was the first Top 10 hit for which American rap group?

2. Which group made their Top 40 debut in 1980 with the single 'Sleepwalk'?

3. From 1964, what was the title of the only Top 10 song achieved by The Pretty Things?

4. What is the title of Mae Muller's Top 10 hit that represented the UK at the Eurovision Song Contest in 2023?

5. Can you name the group that made the Top 10 in both 1981 and 1992 with 'It Must Be Love'?

6 What was the title of Rod Stewart's 1971 number one album that included the hit songs 'Maggie May' and 'Reason To Believe'?

7 From 1984, what was the title of The Toy Dolls' only Top 40 single?

8 According to their only Top 10 hit, which group was on 'The Road To Nowhere'?

9 In 1981, Modern Romance achieved their first Top 10 single. What was the title?

10 Which 1979 Top 10 song by Kool & The Gang did Atomic Kitten take back into the Top 10 in 2003 (and on which the original hit group featured)?

ANSWERS TO ONE THING LEADS TO ANOTHER

1. Britney Spears 2. '...Baby One More Time' 3. Schoolgirl 4. Barry Blue 5. Toto Coelo 6. Blondie 7. 'The Tide Is High' (full title of Atomic Kitten version 'The Tide Is High (Get The Feeling)' 8. Paul Jones 9. Ocean Colour Scene 10. Chelsea F.C. (billed as 'The Chelsea Football Team')

STUCK ON TWO

All these songs reached number two in the charts, but can you remember the song and chart act that stopped them reaching pole position?

1. 'I Swear' by All-4-One
2. 'A Little Bit More' by Dr Hook
3. 'Ghostbusters' by Ray Parker Jr
4. 'The Floral Dance' by Brighouse & Rastrick Brass Band
5. 'Bad Day' by Daniel Powter

6 'No Tears Left To Cry' by Ariana Grande

7 'Penny Lane/Strawberry Fields Forever' by The Beatles

8 'Rule The World' by Take That

9 'You Sexy Thing' by Hot Chocolate

10 'Justified & Ancient' (Lead Vocals by 'The First Lady of Country Music' Miss Tammy Wynette) by The KLF

ANSWERS TO WHO AM I?

1. Run-D.M.C. 2. Ultravox 3. 'Don't Bring Me Down' 4. 'I Wrote A Song' 5. Madness 6. *Every Picture Tells A Story* 7. 'Nellie The Elephant' 8. Talking Heads 9. 'Ay Ay Ay Ay Moosey' 10. 'Ladies Night' (billed as Atomic Kitten featuring Kool & The Gang)
Chart act: Rudimental

SAME TITLE, DIFFERENT SONG

Here are the names of two chart acts who have had different hit songs that share the same title. What is that title?

1. The Ronettes and Vanessa Paradis

2. Chic and Roll Deep

3. Dickie Valentine and Bananarama

4. Eternal and Boyzone

5. Taio Cruz and BTS

6 Public Image Ltd and Gabrielle

7 P!nk and Brandy

8 Don Partridge and Elton John

9 Mariah Carey and Bobby Goldsboro

10 Tears For Fears and ABBA

ANSWERS TO STUCK ON TWO

1.'Love Is All Around' by Wet Wet Wet ('I Swear' spent seven weeks stuck at No. 2.) 2.'Don't Go Breaking My Heart' by Elton John & Kiki Dee ('A Little Bit More' spent five weeks stuck at No. 2.) 3.'I Just Called To Say I Love You' by Stevie Wonder 4.'Mull Of Kintyre/Girls School' by Wings ('The Floral Dance' spent six weeks stuck at No. 2.) 5.'You're Beautiful' by James Blunt 6.'One Kiss' by Calvin Harris & Dua Lipa 7.'Release Me' by Engelbert Humperdinck 8.'Bleeding Love' by Leona Lewis ('Rule The World' spent a month stuck at No. 2.) 9.'Bohemian Rhapsody' by Queen 10.'Bohemian Rhapsody/These Are The Days Of Our Lives' by Queen

DOUBLE A-SIDES

All these records were released as double A-sides, can you name the missing title?

1. 'A Message To You Rudy' by The Specials
2. 'David Watts' by The Jam
3. 'Little Bird' by Annie Lennox
4. 'King' by UB40
5. 'Angeleyes' by ABBA

6 'The Last Goodbye' by Atomic Kitten

7 'Confusion' by Electric Light Orchestra

8 'Get Over You' by Sophie Ellis-Bextor

9 'One Night' by Elvis Presley

10 'In Dulce Jubilo' by Mike Oldfield

ANSWERS TO SAME TITLE, DIFFERENT SONG

1. 'Be My Baby' 2. 'Good Times' 3. 'Venus' 4. 'So Good'
5. 'Dynamite' 6. 'Rise' 7. 'What About Us' 8. 'Blue Eyes'
9. 'Honey' 10. 'Head Over Heels'

1. 'Iron Lion Zion' was a Top 5 song in 1992 for which chart act?
2. What was the name of the band that had a Top 40 single in 1991 with 'You Belong In Rock 'N' Roll'?
3. What type of '_____ Girl' did 3 Colours Red sing about on the group's 1997 Top 30 hit?
4. Freda Payne spent six weeks at number one in 1970 with which song?
5. Which Canadian band had hits in 2002 with 'How You Remind Me', 'Never Again' and 'Too Bad'?
6. What was the title of the last of four number one hits by T.Rex?

7 Can you name the British DJ and performer who made the Top 40 in 2000 with '138 Trek'?

8 On which record label did the hits 'Sunshine Day' by Osibisa, 'Ace Of Spades' by Motorhead and 'Davy's On The Road Again' by Manfred Mann's Earth Band appear?

9 Jim Diamond achieved two solo Top 5 hits during the eighties. The first was his number one 'I Should Have Known Better', but what was the title of the other?

10 From 2002, 'The Dark Is Rising' became the only single to reach the Top 20 for which American rock band?

ANSWERS TO DOUBLE A-SIDES

1. 'Nite Klub' 2. ''A' Bomb In Wardour Street' 3. 'Love Song For A Vampire' 4. 'Food For Thought' 5. 'Voulez-Vous' 6. 'Be With You' 7. 'Last Train To London' 8. 'Move This Mountain' 9. 'I Got Stung' 10. 'On Horseback'

NOT MY SONG

Thinking caps for this one! Here are ten Top 40 acts who might not have the most prolific chart careers, but they are still hitmakers. But one of the three songs isn't theirs. Can you spot which song, and for an extra point, name the chart act that recorded the red herring!

1. Jade: 'I Wanna Love You', 'Don't Walk Away', 'Friend Of Mine'

2. Princess: 'There's Gotta Be More To Life', 'After The Love Has Gone', 'I'll Keep On Loving You'

3. Maneskin: 'I Wanna Be Your Slave', 'Beggin', 'Miserere'

4. Los Bravos: 'I Don't Care', 'Black Is Black', 'Dear Mrs Applebee'

5. Lauryn Hill: 'Everything Is Everything', 'When You Look At Me', 'Ex-Factor'

6 Milk Inc: 'Champagne Dance', 'In My Eyes', 'Land Of The Living'

7 The Peddlers: 'Birth', 'Big Time Operator', 'Girlie'

8 Ella Henderson: 'Glow', 'Chandelier', 'Yours'

9 Patrick Juvet: 'I Love America', 'Got A Feeling', 'Don't Throw It All Away'

10 Felix: 'Shake You Down', 'Don't You Want Me', 'It Will Make Me Crazy'

ANSWERS TO HEAVY METAL

1. Bob Marley and the Wailers 2. Tin Machine 3. 'Copper Girl' 4. 'Band Of Gold' 5. Nickelback 6. 'Metal Guru' 7. DJ Zinc (aka Benjamin Pettit) 8. Bronze 9. 'Hi Ho Silver' 10. Mercury Rev

MIX & MATCH – HITS AND PRODUCERS

Here are ten hit songs followed by ten producers who produced or co-produced the hits.

Can you match the hits with the producers?

HITS

1 'Puss 'N' Boots' by Adam Ant
2 'Rehab' by Amy Winehouse
3 'She's So Beautiful' by Cliff Richard
4 'Something In The Air' by Thunderclap Newman
5 'Family Affair' by Mary J Blige
6 'You Got It' by Roy Orbison
7 'Viva La Vida' by Coldplay
8 'Don't Be Cruel' by Bobby Brown
9 'Have I The Right' by The Honeycombs
10 'Stomp' by Brothers Johnson

PRODUCERS

1. Jeff Lynne
2. Joe Meek
3. Pete Townshend
4. Brian Eno
5. Quincy Jones
6. Dr Dre
7. Babyface
8. Mark Ronson
9. Stevie Wonder
10. Phil Collins

ANSWERS TO NOT MY SONG

1. 'Friend Of Mine' is by Kelly Price. 2. 'There's Gotta Be More To Life' is by Stacie Orrico. 3. 'Miserere' is by Zucchero with Luciano Pavarotti. 4. 'Dear Mrs Applebee' is by David Garrick. 5. 'When You Look At Me' is by Christina Milian. 6. 'Champagne Dance' is by Pay As U Go. 7. 'Big Time Operator' is by Zoot Money and the Big Roll Band. 8. 'Chandelier' is by Sia. 9. 'Don't Throw It All Away' is by Gary Benson (Andy Gibb's song was called '(Our Love) Don't Throw It All Away'.). 10. 'Shake You Down' is by Gregory Abbott.

MIX & MATCH – SONGS AND WRITERS

Here are ten hit songs followed by ten songwriters (and Top 40 artists themselves) who wrote or co-wrote the hits. Can you match the hits with the composers?

HITS

1. 'He's A Rebel' by The Crystals
2. 'Forget You' by CeeLo Green
3. 'Love Me For A Reason' by The Osmonds
4. 'Little Things' by One Direction
5. 'Pink Cadillac' by Natalie Cole
6. 'Hot In Here' by Nelly
7. 'I'll Never Fall In Love Again' by Tom Jones
8. 'I Feel For You' by Chaka Khan
9. 'Chained To The Rhythm' by Katy Perry
10. 'Each Time You Break My Heart' by Nick Kamen

SONGWRITERS

1 Prince
2 Pharrell Williams
3 Gene Pitney
4 Lonnie Donegan
5 Sia
6 Ed Sheeran
7 Bruce Springsteen
8 Madonna
9 Johnny Bristol
10 Bruno Mars

ANSWERS TO MIX & MATCH - HITS AND PRODUCERS

1. 'Puss 'N' Boots' by Adam Ant was produced by Phil Collins. 2. 'Rehab' by Amy Winehouse was produced by Mark Ronson. 3. 'She's So Beautiful' by Cliff Richard was produced by Stevie Wonder. 4. 'Something In The Air' by Thunderclap Newman was produced by Pete Townshend. 5. 'Family Affair' by Mary J Blige was produced by Dr Dre. 6. 'You Got It' by Roy Orbison was produced by Jeff Lynne. 7. 'Viva La Vida' by Coldplay was co-produced by Brian Eno. 8. 'Don't Be Cruel' by Bobby Brown was co-produced by Babyface. 9. 'Have I The Right' by The Honeycombs was produced by Joe Meek. 10. 'Stomp' by Brothers Johnson was produced by Quincy Jones.

ANAGRAMS

Can you work out the titles of these hits in anagram form. As before, the number of anagram words may not be the same as the number of words in the song title!

1. 'Ant Drowns Tot' by Dua Lipa
(*answer includes one apostrophe*)

2. 'Floaty Mahler' by ABC

3. 'Donate Monday' by Suzi Quatro

4. 'Beethoven Command What' by The Script
(*answer includes one apostrophe*)

5. 'Defensive Glows Soothe' by Tears For Fears

6 'Rhetorical Navvies' by The Seekers

7 'Daily Humming Toilette' by Smokie (*answer includes one apostrophe*)

8 'Weeny Hairs' by Enya

9 'Tabatha Blasts Lou' by Meghan Trainor

10 'Charlie Patting Shell' by Lisa Stansfield

ANSWERS TO MIX & MATCH – SONGS AND WRITERS

1. 'He's A Rebel' by The Crystals was written by Gene Pitney.
2. 'Forget You', by CeeLo Green was co-written by Bruno Mars.
3. 'Love Me For A Reason' by The Osmonds was written by Johnny Bristol. 4. 'Little Things' by One Direction was co-written by Ed Sheeran. 5. 'Pink Cadillac' by Natalie Cole was written by Bruce Springsteen. 6. 'Hot In Here' by Nelly was co-written by Pharrell Williams. 7. 'I'll Never Fall In Love Again' by Tom Jones was co-written by Lonnie Donegan. 8. 'I Feel For You' by Chaka Khan was written by Prince. 9. 'Chained To The Rhythm' by Katy Perry was co-written by Sia. 10. 'Each Time You Break My Heart' by Nick Kamen was co-written by Madonna.

MY LIFE STORY

Can you work out who these singers are from these brief biographies?

1 I was born in New York in the 1940s and during the 1970s I was married to James Taylor. My hit singles include songs that appeared in the films *Heartburn* and *The Spy Who Loved Me*, and my song 'Let The River Run' was the theme to the film *Working Girl*.

2 I was born in Bedford in 1995. I was briefly a youth player at Luton Town Football Club. I studied acting at university in Twickenham, but also gigged around London. I had my first Top 10 single in 2021 with 'Little Bit Of Love' and my albums *Evering Road* and *What Ifs & Maybes* both entered the chart at number one.

3

I was born in Southampton in 1981. My first chart appearance was as the vocalist on a 1999 single by Artful Dodger. In 2000 I became the youngest British male artist to write and record a number one single and my debut album *Born To Do It* sold over 1.5 million copies in the UK.

4

I was born in Sydney in 1975. Having appeared in *Neighbours*, I launched my pop career in 1997 with the multi-platinum album *Left Of The Middle*. I starred alongside Rowan Atkinson in the film *Johnny English* and appeared on the UK version of *The Masked Singer* in 2022 as Panda.

5

I was born in Glasgow in 1946. I was dubbed the British Bob Dylan in the 1960s and my hits include 'There Is A Mountain' and 'Goo Goo Barabajagal (Love Is Hot)'.

CONTINUES OVERLEAF

6 I was born in California in 2003. I starred in the TV show *High School Musical: The Musical: The Series*. In 2021, my debut album *Sour* entered the chart at number one and contained two number one singles that same year. In 2023 I had a big hit with the song 'Vampire'.

7 I was born in Birmingham in 1948. I've sung with The Spencer Davis Group, Traffic and Blind Faith and although they just missed the Top 40, some of my best-known solo songs from the eighties are 'While You See A Chance' and 'Roll With It'.

8 I was born in New York City in 1985. My real name is Elizabeth Woolridge Grant, but my stage name is said to be inspired by both a film star of the 1940s and 1950s and a make of car. I had both a Top 10 single and number one album in 2012 called *Born To Die*.

9 I was born in Middlesbrough in 1951. My debut hit single in 1978 was also a hit for Elkie Brooks in 1982. My Top 10 albums include *God's Great Banana Skin* and *Auberge* and my final Top 40 single of the 20th century was called 'You Can Go Your Own Way'.

10 I was born Walden Robert Cassotto in New York in 1936 and died in 1973. My first UK hit was 'Splish Splash' in 1958 and I had my first number one the following year with 'Dream Lover'. My last Top 10 hit came in 1966 with a version of Tim Hardin's song, 'If I Were A Carpenter'.

ANSWERS TO ANAGRAMS

1. 'Don't Start Now' 2. 'All Of My Heart' 3. 'Daytona Demon' 4. 'The Man Who Can't Be Moved' 5. 'Sowing The Seeds Of Love' 6. 'The Carnival Is Over' 7. 'I'll Meet You At Midnight' 8. 'Anywhere Is' 9. 'All About That Bass' 10. 'In All The Right Places'

ONE FOR THE ALBUM

Below are the first and last tracks of UK number one albums along with the year they reached number one (which might not be the year of release!). Can you name the album and who recorded it? Tracks are from the standard original release, not deluxe or expanded editions and are certified platinum or multi-platinum albums.

1. 'Come Back & Stay' and 'Sex' - 1983
2. 'Death On Two Legs (Dedicated To...)' and 'God Save The Queen' - 1975
3. 'The Greatest Show' and 'From Now On' - 2018
4. 'I Still Do' and 'Put Me Down' - 1994
5. 'One' and 'Afire Love' - 2014

6. 'Honey' and 'My Weakness' - 2000

7. 'Watch That Man' and 'Lady Grinning Soul' - 1973

8. 'Hung Up' and 'Like It Or Not' - 2005

9. 'The Boy In The Bubble' and 'All Around The World or The Myth of Fingerprints' - 1986

10. 'Drive' and 'Find The River' - 1992

ANSWERS TO MY LIFE STORY

1. Carly Simon 2. Tom Grennan 3. Craig David 4. Natalie Imbruglia 5. Donovan 6. Olivia Rodrigo 7. Steve Winwood 8. Lana Del Rey (Lana Turner, Ford Del Rey) 9. Chris Rea 10. Bobby Darin

MISSING WORDS

What is the missing word that completes these Top 40 song titles?

1. '_____ On The Beach' by Taylor Swift featuring Lana Del Rey

2. 'Broken Down _____' by Nazareth

3. 'I'll Be Loving You (_____)' by New Kids On The Block

4. 'The _____ Time' by Kim Wilde

5. 'Hold My _____' by George Ezra

6 'My ____ Lover' by Chic

7 'I'm Gonna Be ____' by Jennifer Lopez

8 '____ Is Contagious' by Taja Sevelle

9 'The ____ Man' by Detroit Spinners

10 'Transfer ____' by A Flock Of Seagulls

ANSWERS TO ONE FOR THE ALBUM

1. *No Parlez* by Paul Young 2. *A Night At The Opera* by Queen 3. *The Greatest Showman* the original motion picture soundtrack 4. *Everybody Else Is Doing It So Why Can't We* by The Cranberries (originally released 1993) 5. *X* by Ed Sheeran 6. *Play* by Moby (originally released in 1999) 7. *Aladdin Sane* by David Bowie 8. *Confessions On A Dance Floor* by Madonna 9. *Graceland* by Paul Simon 10. *Automatic For The People* by R.E.M.

WHO AM I?

The first letter of each answer to the questions below spells out the name of which chart act?

1. Released in 1961, what was the title of the Top 3 instrumental by Mr Acker Bilk that spent a total of 52 weeks in the Top 40?

2. Lulu was featured on the 1993 number one 'Relight My Fire' by which successful vocal group?

3. What was the title of the 1956 Top 20 hit by Dick James with Stephen James and His Chums and Ron Goodwin's Orchestra, which was also the theme song to a successful television series?

4. Can you name the actor and singer who made the Top 10 in 1999 with 'I Breathe Again'?

5. What was the title of the first single by Bad Manners to make the Top 40?

6 Who reached the Top 5 in 1990 with 'Infinity (1990s . . . Time For The Guru)'?

7 From 1968, 'Everlasting Love' was the first and only number one achieved by which group?

8 What was the title of the 1971 number one album by T.Rex that included their hits 'Get It On' and 'Jeepster'?

9 The song 'Black Betty' was Top 10 in 1977 and also a Top 20 remix in 1990 for which group?

10 What was the title of the 2019 number one duet by Shawn Mendes and Camila Cabello?

ANSWERS TO MISSING WORDS

1. 'SNOW On The Beach' 2. 'Broken Down ANGEL' 3. 'I'll Be Loving You (FOREVER)' 4. 'The SECOND Time' 5. 'Hold My GIRL' 6. 'My FORBIDDEN Lover' 7. 'I'm Gonna Be ALRIGHT' 8. 'LOVE Is Contagious' 9. 'The RUBBERBAND Man' 10. 'Transfer AFFECTION'

POPMASTER – THE GOLDEN YEARS

Welcome to 'PopMaster – The Golden Years'. Over the next three sections we have a range of questions on three decades of music: the 1970s, 1980s and 1990s.

Each section is split into three parts. There are ten sets of questions that cover the whole of each decade, followed by ten sets that might be a little more challenging as they focus on each individual year (1970, 1971, 1972, etc.). Then to round things off, five sets of questions, each concentrating on one of five successful acts who made their chart debut in that particular decade. The questions, though, cover the whole of their careers.

Have fun!

1970s GOLDEN YEARS

Flares, safety pins, kipper ties, platforms and clogs, *Tiswas, Timeslip, The Tomorrow People, Runaround* and *Here Come The Double Deckers*!

1970s POPMASTER 1

1. Who reached number one in 1972 with the song 'School's Out'?

2. Which Bob Marley song became a Top 10 hit for Eric Clapton in 1974?

3. Can you name the punk group that made their chart debut in 1978 with the song 'The Day The World Turned Dayglo' and who sang lead vocals on the track?

4. The band The Hotshots made its only chart appearance in 1973 with which Top 5 single?

5. What is the name of the duo that had hits in 1979 called 'Who Were You With In The Moonlight' and 'Love's Gotta Hold On Me'?

6. Which backing group is billed alongside Archie Bell on the seventies hits 'The Soul City Walk' and 'Here I Go Again'?

7 'He's So Fine', 'One Fine Day' and 'Sweet Talkin' Guy' were all hits in the sixties for The Chiffons. Which one was re-issued in 1972 and became a Top 5 single?

8 The 1978 hit 'You Make Me Feel (Mighty Real)' was the only Top 10 single for which disco artist?

9 What is the name of the family group that had Top 10 singles in the late seventies with the songs 'Wanted' and 'The Chosen Few'?

10 Genesis first reached the Top 40 in 1974 with a single subtitled '(In Your Wardrobe)'. What is its full title?

ANSWERS TO WHO AM I?

1. 'Stranger On The Shore' 2. Take That 3. 'Robin Hood' (jointly listed with 'The Ballad Of Davy Crockett' which was on the other side) 4. Adam Rickett 5. 'Ne-Ne Na-Na Na-Na Nu-Nu' 6. Guru Josh 7. Love Affair 8. *Electric Warrior* 9. Ram Jam 10. 'Senorita'
Chart Act: Stranglers

1970s POPMASTER 2

1. What type of '_____ Holiday' did 10cc take, according to the title of the group's 1978 number one?

2. In 1976, 'It Should Have Been Me' was a Top 5 single and the only Top 40 appearance for Yvonne _____ who?

3. Teach-In won the Eurovision Song Contest for The Netherlands in 1975 with which Top 20 song?

4. 'Young, Gifted and Black' was a Top 5 hit in 1970 for which Jamaican duo?

5. Which American singer's solo hits in the seventies included 'You're Ready Now', 'Swearin' To God' and 'Fallen Angel'?

6 Released in 1979, what is the title of the only UK number one by Dr Hook?

7 Which group had a hit with the song 'Beach Baby' in 1974?

8 The theme tune to one of the biggest films in the mid-seventies was turned into a 1976 hit by the Argentine arranger and conductor Lalo Schifrin. What was the film?

9 Which band was 'Accident Prone' according to the title of their 1978 Top 40 single?

10 Dr Feelgood had three Top 40 singles in the seventies, 1979's Top 10 hit 'Milk And Alcohol' was one of them. Can you name one of the other two?

ANSWERS TO 1970s POPMASTER 1

1. Alice Cooper 2. 'I Shot The Sheriff' 3. X-Ray Spex - Poly Styrene 4. 'Snoopy vs The Red Baron' 5. Dollar 6. The Drells 7. 'Sweet Talkin' Guy' 8. Sylvester 9. The Dooleys 10. 'I Know What I Like (In Your Wardrobe)'

1970s POPMASTER 3

1. In 1976, Leo Sayer sang 'You Make Me Feel Like _____' what?

2. Which group made their chart debut in 1972 with the song 'Ball Park Incident'?

3. Diana Ross had her first solo number one in 1971 with a song that spent a month at the top of the charts. What was it called?

4. The songs 'Money Honey', 'Summerlove Sensation', and 'Love Me Like I Love You' were all Top 5 songs in the mid-seventies for which group?

5. What was the title of the Johnny Mathis and Deniece Williams duet that reached the Top 3 in 1978?

6 In 1979, the song 'King Rocker' became the highest charting single in the career of which punk band?

7 Complete the title of this 1972 Top 10 single by Johnny Nash: 'There Are More ____' what?

8 'This Is Tomorrow' and 'Tokyo Joe' were both solo singles in 1977 for which singer?

9 Which American vocal group recorded the 1971 hits 'Didn't I (Blow Your Mind This Time)' and 'La-La Means I Love You'?

10 In 1975, 'Funky Moped' was one track on a Top 5 double A-side by the comedian Jasper Carrott. What is the title of the AA-side?

ANSWERS TO 1970s POPMASTER 2

1. 'Dreadlock Holiday' 2. Yvonne Fair 3. 'Ding-A-Dong' 4. Bob and Marcia 5. Frankie Valli 6. 'When You're In Love With A Beautiful Woman' 7. First Class 8. *Jaws* 9. Status Quo 10. 'She's A Wind Up' (No. 34 in 1977), 'As Long As The Price Is Right' (No. 40 in 1979)

1970s POPMASTER 4

1. Barry White had his only UK number one single in 1974 with which song?

2. Which group reached the Top 10 in 1970 with 'The Green Manalishi (With The Two-Prong Crown)'?

3. What is the title of the 1977 Top 10 instrumental by The Rah Band?

4. Who was 'Lost In France' according to the title of her 1976 debut chart appearance?

5. Jimmy Helms had his only solo hit in 1973 with which Top 10 song?

6 In 1974, which American chart act asked 'Who's In The Strawberry Patch With Sally'?

7 The band Funkadelic made their only chart appearance in the late seventies with which Top 10 single?

8 Which British singer-songwriter had both of his Top 40 hits in the first half of the seventies with the songs 'Gaye' and 'Scullery'?

9 What '_____ Boy' did guitarist George Benson sing about on his 1977 single?

10 Which folk singer sang lead vocals on Steeleye Span's hits 'Gaudete' and 'All Around My Hat'?

ANSWERS TO 1970s POPMASTER 3

1. 'You Make Me Feel Like Dancing' 2. Wizzard 3. 'I'm Still Waiting' 4. Bay City Rollers 5. 'Too Much, Too Little, Too Late' 6. Generation X 7. 'There Are More Questions Than Answers' 8. Bryan Ferry 9. The Delfonics 10. 'Magic Roundabout'

1970s POPMASTER 5

1. Which punk group was 'Pretty Vacant' in 1977?

2. Roy Wood had four solo Top 40 hits in the seventies. 'Forever' was one of them. Can you name one of the other three?

3. The songs 'Heaven Help Us All', 'If You Really Love Me' and 'We Can Work It Out' were all hits in the early seventies for which artist?

4. The Top 40 song 'Third Finger Left Hand' in 1972 and the Top 10 hit 'Guilty' in 1974 were both hits for which female vocal duo?

5. What '_____ Cowboy' did Mike Harding sing about on his 1975 single?

6 The songs 'Love Me Like A Lover', 'Dr. Love' and 'Love Bug' all reached the Top 40 in the second half of the seventies for which singer?

7 Which group sang about 'The Witch Queen Of New Orleans' on their 1971 Top 3 hit?

8 What is the only Top 40 single in the seventies by Roxy Music whose title doesn't feature in the lyrics of the song?

9 Having left The Temptations, Eddie Kendricks had two solo hit singles in the first half of the seventies. Can you name either of them?

10 What 1979 hit by The Stranglers has a noble title?

ANSWERS TO 1970s POPMASTER 4

1. 'You're The First, The Last, My Everything' 2. Fleetwood Mac 3. 'The Crunch' (Officially 'The Crunch (Part 1)' as the 'B' side was 'The Crunch (Part 2)'.) 4. Bonnie Tyler 5. 'Gonna Make You An Offer You Can't Refuse' (Jimmy would have hits in the late 1980s/ early 1990s as a member of Londonbeat.) 6. Dawn featuring Tony Orlando 7. 'One Nation Under A Groove (Part 1)' 8. Clifford T. Ward 9. 'Nature Boy' 10. Maddy Prior

1970s POPMASTER 6

1. Two of the Top 10 singles by Showaddywaddy in the seventies had one-word titles. 'Heartbeat' was one. What was the other?

2. In 1971, Lobo sang about 'Me And You And A ____' what?

3. What is the name of the band that featured alongside Jonathan Richman on the 1977 Top 5 hit 'Egyptian Reggae'?

4. Can you name the group that made the Top 20 in 1978 with the song 'Top Of The Pops'?

5. What was the only single by Meat Loaf to reach the Top 20 during the seventies?

6 In 1975, The Sensational Alex Harvey Band reached the charts with a live version of a Tom Jones hit from 1968. What is the song?

7 What is the name of the group whose first Top 20 hit was a 1970 cover of the Led Zeppelin classic 'Whole Lotta Love'?

8 'Sugar Baby Love' was number one for the Rubettes in 1974. What was the title of the group's Top 20 follow-up hit?

9 Which brother and sister act topped the album charts in 1975 with *Horizon*?

10 Who was the female singer featured on Eruption's 1978 Top 5 version of the song 'I Can't Stand The Rain'?

ANSWERS TO 1970s POPMASTER 5

1. The Sex Pistols 2. 'Dear Elaine' (1973), 'Goin' Down The Road (A Scottish Reggae Song)' (1974), 'Oh What A Shame' (1975) 3. Stevie Wonder 4. The Pearls 5. 'Rochdale Cowboy' 6. Tina Charles 7. Redbone 8. 'Pyjamarama' 9. 'Keep On Truckin'' (1973), 'Boogie Down' (1974) 10. 'Duchess'

1970s POPMASTER 7

1. What was the title of the only hit by Hotlegs before they re-emerged as 10cc?

2. What words follow in brackets on the 1978 Top 10 song by Leo Sayer, 'I Can't Stop Loving You'?

3. From 1979, what was the title of Bill Lovelady's only UK hit?

4. Who wrote David Cassidy's 1975 Top 20 single, 'I Write The Songs'?

5. The Beach Boys achieved two Top 10 hits during the seventies. The first was 'Cottonfields', what was the other?

6 What was the title of Lene Lovich's Top 20 follow-up to her Top 5 debut, 'Lucky Number'?

7 Which singer-songwriter released the 1975 album *Still Crazy After All These Years*?

8 What was the title of the first single by Squeeze to make the Top 40?

9 What was the name of the group that featured Paul Young on vocals and had a double A-side hit in 1978 with 'Toast' and 'Hold On'?

10 Can you name the group that had Top 20 hits in the first half of the seventies with 'What's Your Name' and 'Good Grief Christina'?

ANSWERS TO 1970s POPMASTER 6

1. 'When' 2. 'Me And You And A Dog Named Boo' 3. The Modern Lovers 4. The Rezillos 5. 'Bat Out Of Hell' (it became a Top 10 hit when it was re-issued in 1993.) 6. 'Delilah' 7. C.C.S. 8. 'Tonight' 9. The Carpenters 10. Precious Wilson

1970s POPMASTER 8

1. Can you name the group that had Top 10 songs in the early seventies called 'Tom-Tom Turnaround' and 'Sister Jane'?

2. Having reached number one in 1969 with 'I'll Never Fall In Love Again', which other Bacharach and David song gave Bobbie Gentry her only Top 40 solo hit in the seventies?

3. Who wrote Bryan Ferry's 1973 Top 10 single 'A Hard Rain's A-Gonna Fall'?

4. From 1978, which Australian singer achieved her only Top 20 hit with 'Emotion'?

5. What was the title of the first Top 20 single by The Jam?

6. Which chart act topped the album charts for one week in 1979 with *Replicas*?

7 The songs 'Music' and 'Slow Down' were both Top 10 singles by John Miles in the seventies, but he had two other Top 40 hits during the decade. Can you name either of these?

8 In 1978, which American country group wanted to 'Kiss You All Over'?

9 Which three words in brackets precede 'I'm The One You Need' in the title of the 1971 Top 20 song by Smokey Robinson and The Miracles?

10 Can you name the 1977 Top 20 single by The Trammps that became a Top 20 cover for Tina Turner in the nineties?

ANSWERS TO 1970s POPMASTER 7

1. 'Neanderthal Man' 2. 'I Can't Stop Loving You (Though I Try)' 3. 'Reggae For It Now' 4. Bruce Johnston 5. 'Lady Lynda' 6. 'Say When' 7. Paul Simon 8. 'Take Me I'm Yours' 9. Streetband 10. Chicory Tip

1970s POPMASTER 9

1 Which legendary rock band had a 'Mystery Song' in the Top 20 in 1976?

2 In 1979, Boney M made the Top 10 with their cover of a 1966 Top 40 single by The Creation. Can you name the song?

3 Who wrote Rita Coolidge's 1977 Top 10 hit, 'We're All Alone'?

4 What was the name of the Tottenham Hotspur football supporter who made the Top 20 in 1973 with 'Nice One Cyril'?

5 Candi Staton reached the Top 10 on two occasions during the seventies. The first being 'Young Hearts Run Free'. What was the title of the second one?

6 Who topped the album charts in 1973 with *Billion Dollar Babies*?

7 In 1977, The Stranglers made the Top 10 with their double A-side 'Something Better Change' and which other song?

8 Journalist Paul Phillips achieved a Top 10 hit in the late seventies called 'Car 67'. Under what name did he release the record?

9 The songs 'Used Ta Be My Girl', 'Brandy' and a re-issue of 'I Love Music' were all hits in 1978 for which American soul group?

10 Who were the Boomtown Rats 'Lookin' After _____' according to the title of the group's 1977 chart debut?

ANSWERS TO 1970s POPMASTER 8

1. New World 2. 'Raindrops Keep Fallin' On My Head' 3. Bob Dylan 4. Samantha Sang (Some pressings of the single had the title as 'Emotions'.) 5. 'All Around The World' 6. Tubeway Army 7. 'Highfly' (Top 20 chart debut in 1975) 'Remember Yesterday' (Top 40 follow-up to 'Music'.) 8. Exile 9. '(Come Round Here) I'm The One You Need' 10. 'Disco Inferno'

1970s POPMASTER 10

1. Which chart act had a Top 3 single in 1979 with 'Pop Muzik'?

2. Which Paul McCartney song gave Billy Paul a 1977 Top 40 hit?

3. In 1971, Elvis Presley made the Top 10 with a double A-side re-issue of two of his Top 3 hits from 1956, 'Heartbreak Hotel' and which other song?

4. Which 1962 Top 3 hit by Brian Hyland returned to the Top 10 in 1975?

5. *Hergest Ridge* was a 1974 number one album for which multi-instrumentalist?

6 Released in 1972, The Partridge Family's Top 20 hit 'It's One Of Those Nights' has two words in brackets at the end of its title. What are those two words?

7 What was the last single to reach number one in the seventies and who recorded it?

8 Which singer-songwriter composed The New Seekers' 1972 Top 5 hit 'Circles'?

9 In 1979, The Sex Pistols made the Top 3 with the double A-side 'Something Else' and which other song?

10 Which Australian singer had his only UK Top 10 single in 1978 with 'Love Is In The Air'?

ANSWERS TO 1970s POPMASTER 9

1. Status Quo 2. 'Painter Man' 3. Boz Scaggs 4. Cockerel Chorus 5. 'Nights On Broadway' 6. Alice Cooper 7. 'Straighten Out' 8. Driver 67 9. The O'Jays 10. 'Lookin' After No. 1'

1970

1. Officially billed as Dave Edmund's Rockpile (though on some copies just Dave Edmunds), which number one was a cover of a fifties song recorded by Smiley Lewis?

2. Badfinger had a Top 5 hit in January this year with 'Come And Get It'. Which Beatle both wrote and produced the single?

3. The group Pickettywitch had all three of its chart hits this year. 'Baby I Won't Let You Down' was the last of these. Can you name one of the other two?

4. Who released a number one double album this year called *Self Portrait* which, not surprisingly, featured a self-portrait of the singer-songwriter on the cover?

5. Lee Marvin's number one 'Wandrin' Star' featured in a film that also starred Clint Eastwood and Jean Seberg. What was it called?

6. Steven Tyler, Joe Perry, Tom Hamilton and Joey Kramer were all original members of which band formed this year?

7 In 1970, the American band Frijid Pink had their only UK hit with a Top 5 version of a song that had been a number one in the sixties. What is the song?

8 France, Netherlands, Spain and the United Kingdom all tied on the same number of points to win the 1969 Eurovision Song Contest. But which of these four countries hosted the 1970 competition, where Dana won for Ireland with 'All Kinds Of Everything'?

9 Black Sabbath's chart debut in the summer of 1970 would also be the only Top 10 single in the band's chart career. What was it called?

10 What are the first names of Crosby, Stills, Nash and Young, whose 1970 album *Déjà Vu* has sold over 7 million copies in America?

ANSWERS TO 1970s POPMASTER 10

1. M 2. 'Let 'Em In' 3. 'Hound Dog' 4. 'Sealed With A Kiss' 5. Mike Oldfield 6. 'It's One Of Those Nights (Yes Love)' 7. 'Another Brick In The Wall Part II' by Pink Floyd 8. Harry Chapin 9. 'Friggin' In The Riggin'' 10. John Paul Young

1971

1. The Sweet had a hit this year singing about which Scottish-born inventor?

2. In 1971, which American vocal group had their only two UK chart hits with 'Put Yourself In My Place' and 'Heaven Must Have Sent You'?

3. Scott English reached the charts with a song that would go on to be a hit as 'Mandy' for both Barry Manilow and Westlife. But what was the title of Scott's Top 20 single?

4. Vernie Bennett was born in May this year. With which vocal group did she have twelve Top 10 hits in the nineties?

5. What type of '_____ Love' did The Supremes sing about on their Top 3 single?

6. One of the biggest films at the UK box office in 1971 was *Soldier Blue*. In the late summer, its theme song became a Top 10 hit for its writer. Who is she?

7 Which chart act is credited with recording this year's novelty hit 'Leap Up And Down (Wave Your Knickers In The Air)'?

8 What is the title of the live album by Emerson Lake & Palmer that is a rock adaptation of the music of Modest Mussorgsky?

9 The first series of *The Two Ronnies* aired in 1971 and featured, as regular musical guests, a vocal group from Australia who were in the charts with 'Rose Garden' as the series started. What is the name of the group?

10 Having spent seven weeks at number one in 1970 with 'In The Summertime', Mungo Jerry spent a more modest two weeks at number one this year with their second and final chart topper. What was it called?

ANSWERS TO 1970

1. 'I Hear You Knocking' 2. Paul McCartney 3. 'That Same Old Feeling' (Top 5), '(It's Like A) Sad Old Kinda Movie' (Top 20) 4. Bob Dylan 5. *Paint Your Wagon* 6. Aerosmith 7. 'The House Of The Rising Sun' 8. Netherlands 9. 'Paranoid' 10. Dave Crosby, Stephen Stills, Graham Nash, Neil Young

1972

1. Which group took a 'Supersonic Rocket Ship' on their Top 20 hit in 1972?

2. Which American country music singer had his only UK hit single and album this year, both called 'It's Four In The Morning'?

3. The band Blackfoot Sue made their chart debut with which Top 5 song?

4. Diana Ross made her feature film debut this year in a movie based on the life of Billie Holiday. What was it called?

5. 'Desiderata', a poem written in the 1920s by Max Ehrmann, became a Top 10 spoken word single for an American radio announcer and talk-show host. What was he called?

6. The Greek singer Vicky Leandros won the 1972 Eurovision Song Contest for Luxembourg with the song *'Après Toi'*. What was its English title when it became a Top 3 hit that year?

7. Graham, Paul, Kristian, Layton and Doyle are the surnames of the members of one of the

most popular vocal groups of 1972. What is the name of the group?

8 The Fortunes had their final hit this year with the Top 10 single 'Storm In A Teacup'. It was co-written by someone who would make her chart debut later in the year with the song 'Sugar Me'. Who is she?

9 Released towards the end of 1971, The John Barry Orchestra reached the Top 20 in January 1972 with the theme tune to a TV series starring Roger Moore and Tony Curtis. What was it called?

10 During the height of T.Rex-mania this year, the first two albums by Tyrannosaurus Rex were re-issued as a double album package and reached number one. One of these two albums was called *Prophets, Seers and Sages: The Angels Of The Ages*. What is the title of the other? (Good luck!)

ANSWERS TO 1971

1. 'Alexander Graham Bell' 2. The Elgins (Both singles had originally been hits in the USA in the mid-sixties.) 3. 'Brandy' 4. Eternal 5. 'Stoned Love' ('Baby Love' was 1964) 6. Buffy Sainte-Marie (Film originally released in the USA in August 1970, but became one of the Top 10 box-office hits in the UK in 1971.) 7. St Cecilia (the subtitle was omitted from the label of UK pressings of the single) 8. *Pictures At An Exhibition* 9. New World 10. 'Baby Jump'

1973

1 'Eye Level', the number one by the Simon Park Orchestra, was the theme tune to which television series?

2 Which child singer had a Top 40 hit called 'Let There Be Peace On Earth (Let It Begin With Me)'?

3 In October this year, David Bowie released an album of cover versions called *Pin Ups*. Bryan Ferry entered the charts the same week with his debut solo album that was also comprised of cover versions. What was this called?

4 Prior to their debut hit 'Pick Up The Pieces', the duo Hudson-Ford had been members of which group?

5 Which Top 20 hit for Roger Daltrey has the full official credit of 'Roger Daltrey with the London Symphony Orchestra & English Chamber Choir conducted by David Measham'?

6 Having been an extra in the Beatles' film *A Hard Day's Night*, appeared on stage at the first Glastonbury Festival and sung backing vocals on Cat Stevens' album *Catch Bull At Four*, which

singer-songwriter made her solo chart debut in 1973 with the Top 20 hit 'Rock-A-Doodle-Doo'?

7 What is the title of the film released this year that starred David Essex as Jim MacLaine, Ringo Starr as Mike, Billy Fury as Stormy Tempest and Keith Moon as J.D. Clover?

8 Nazareth had a hit with 'This Flight Tonight' in the closing months of 1973, but who wrote the song?

9 What track closes side one of the original vinyl release of Pink Floyd's *Dark Side Of The Moon*?

10 What were the first names of the duo Peters and Lee, who reached number one with their single 'Welcome Home'?

ANSWERS TO 1972

1. The Kinks 2. Faron Young 3. 'Standing In The Road' 4. 'Lady Sings The Blues' 5. Les Crane 6. 'Come What May' 7. The New Seekers - (No. 1 for the whole of January with 'I'd Like To Teach The World To Sing'; Came second at Eurovision with their Top 3 song 'Beg, Steal Or Borrow' and Top 5 with their single 'Circles') 8. Lynsey De Paul ('Storm In A Teacup' written under her real name, Lyndsey Rubin) 9. 'The Persuaders' 10. 'My People Were Fair And Had Sky In Their Hair . . . But Now They're Content To Wear Stars On Their Brows'

1974

1. 'He's Misstra Know-It-All' was a Top 10 single this year for which American artist?

2. Mud's Top 10 single 'Rocket' was released on RAK Records (RAK 178). Another single released the same month (RAK 179) was also by the group but released under a pseudonym. It was a cover of a tune made famous by Glenn Miller. What is it called and under what name was it released?

3. Which songwriting duo wrote and produced George McCrae's number one 'Rock Your Baby' as well as his other hits this year: 'You Can Have It All' and 'I Can't Leave You Alone'?

4. What music-hall song from the early 1900s can be heard at the end of Queen's debut hit 'Seven Seas Of Rhye'?

5. Kenny released 'The Bump' this year. Prior to it entering the charts, it had been recorded as the B-side of a Top 5 hit by one of the year's biggest pop groups. Can you name that group? (And award yourself an extra point if you know the title of the A-side.)

6 Released in the summer of 1974, what number one album by Elton John was named after the studio where it was partly recorded?

7 'Saturday Gig', the final single from Mott The Hoople, stalled at number 41 but told the story of the band's history. In it, Ian Hunter sings he was ready to call it a day, but a visit to which south London town changed his mind?

8 Andy Kim had a Top 3 solo hit called 'Rock Me Gently' this year. But his biggest international success was as co-songwriter of a number one and one of the biggest selling singles worldwide in 1969. What was that song?

9 The Top 40 instrumental 'Galloping Home' by the London String Chorale was the theme tune to which TV programme?

10 Which soul group from Harlem, New York City, had their only British hit with their American Top 10 song 'Just Don't Want To Be Lonely'?

ANSWERS TO 1973

1. *Van Der Valk* 2. Michael Ward 3. 'These Foolish Things' 4. The Strawbs 5. 'I'm Free' 6. Linda Lewis 7. 'That'll Be The Day' 8. Joni Mitchell 9. 'The Great Gig In The Sky' 10. Lennie Peters and Dianne Lee (Di Lee)

1975

1. A version of which television theme tune was recorded by Wings as the closing track to the number one album *Venus And Mars*?

2. Who was the uncredited lead vocalist on the 5000 Volts single 'I'm On Fire'?

3. In 1975, a year before their number one chart debut 'You To Me Are Everything', members of The Real Thing appeared as backing vocalists on a Top 5 single by David Essex. What was it called?

4. The producer of eighties hits 'Geno' by Dexy's Midnight Runners, 'That Ole Devil Called Love' by Alison Moyet and 'I'm Gonna Be (500 Miles), by The Proclaimers, had his one and only Top 40 hit under his own name in this year. Who is he and what is the title of his Top 10 song?

5. A film starring Slade as members of a fictitious band premiered this year. What was it called?

6. The vocal group Guys and Dolls made their chart debut this year. The sextet included Julie, the daughter of one of the biggest television stars of the day. Who was he?

7 Members of The Eagles, who first reached the UK charts this year with the singles 'One Of These Nights' and 'Lyin' Eyes', had earlier in the seventies been members of the backing band for which American singer?

8 David Cassidy had his final hit of the decade in 1975 with a cover of which Beach Boys song?

9 The song 'Good Lovin' Gone Bad' was a Top 40 hit for a supergroup made up of members of King Crimson, Free and Mott The Hoople. What is the name of the group?

10 Having had a Top 3 hit in 1974 with 'The Man Who Sold The World', Lulu had her only other Top 40 hit of the seventies this year with which song?

ANSWERS TO 1974

1. Stevie Wonder 2. 'In The Mood' by Dum 3. Harry Casey & Rick Finch (from KC and The Sunshine Band) 4. 'I Do Like To Be Beside The Seaside' 5. Bay City Rollers, 'All Of Me Loves All Of You' 6. *Caribou*, partly recorded at the Caribou Ranch in Colorado 7. Croydon 8. 'Sugar, Sugar' by The Archies 9. *The Adventures of Black Beauty* (Single released in 1973, but didn't reach the Top 40. Re-entered chart early in 1974.) 10. The Main Ingredient

1976

1. The duo James and Bobby Purify had both of their hit singles this year. Can you name either of them?

2. The song 'Boston Tea Party' reached the Top 20 in the summer of 1976 for which group?

3. The title of ABBA's number one 'Mamma Mia' appears in the lyrics of the song it knocked off the top spot. What is that song?

4. Having had a run of hits between 1973 and 1975, which singer appeared in a TV 'Green Cross Code' campaign this year called 'Children's Heroes'?

5. The duo R & J Stone made their only Top 40 appearance in 1976 with which Top 5 song?

6. A group of studio musicians calling themselves The Wing And A Prayer Fife And Drum Corps had a Top 20 hit with a largely instrumental version of a jazz song from the 1920s. What was it called?

7 Eric Carmen's song 'All By Myself' has a melody partly based on the music of which of these classical composers: Prokofiev, Rachmaninoff or Shostakovich?

8 Featuring singer Midge Ure, the band Slik had two hit singles this year: the number one 'Forever And Ever' and which Top 30 song?

9 A TV musical drama called *Rock Follies* premiered in 1976. With music by Roxy Music's Andy Mackay, it told the story of The Little Ladies – Devonia (Dee), Anna and Nancy (Q) – a fictional trio trying to make it in the music business. Can you name one of the three actors who played these roles?

10 Donna Summer made her UK chart debut this year with a Top 5 single that was initially deemed a bit too sexy to get airplay. What is the song?

ANSWERS TO 1975

1. 'Crossroads' 2. Tina Charles 3. 'Rolling Stone' 4. Pete Wingfield, 'Eighteen With A Bullet' 5. *Slade in Flame* (The film was released January 1975, the band's soundtrack album had been released November 1974.) 6. Bruce Forsyth 7. Linda Ronstadt 8. 'Darlin' 9. Bad Company 10. 'Take Your Mama For A Ride' (Officially called 'Take Your Mama For A Ride (Part 1)' as '(Part 2)' was on the 'B' side.)

1977

1. Mary Visconti was a backing vocalist on David Bowie's 'Sound And Vision', but by what other name is she well known?

2. *Deceptive Bends* was the first 10cc album following the departure of Lol Creme and Kevin Godley. Which two original members continued with the band name?

3. Danny Williams, who'd had a run of hits in the early sixties, returned to the charts this year with a Top 30 song that had featured in commercials for Martini. What was the single called?

4. Which pop star, with five Top 40 hits in 1973 and 1974, produced Heatwave's 1977 Top 3 debut 'Boogie Nights'?

5. Which singer and which double A-side single stopped 'God Save The Queen' by The Sex Pistols being number one in the week of the Silver Jubilee bank holiday?

6. The saxophone player on Thin Lizzy's 'Dancin' In The Moonlight (It's Caught Me In Its Spotlight)' is John Helliwell, who at the time was a member of which other band?

7 Carole Bayer Sager had her only solo hit this year with the Top 10 single 'You're Moving Out Today'. But she'd reached number one earlier in 1977 as co-writer of a number one by Leo Sayer. What is the song, and who was her co-writer?

8 What are the first names of the twin brothers Alessi, who had a Top 10 hit with 'Oh Lori'?

9 Husband and wife Marilyn McCoo and Billy Davis Jr. reached the Top 10 with 'You Don't Have To Be A Star (To Be In My Show)'. But they'd previously had hits in Britain and America as members of which vocal group?

10 Having had a Top 3 hit in 1976 with 'Jeans On', David Dundas made his only other Top 40 solo appearance in 1977 with which song?

ANSWERS TO 1976

1. 'I'm Your Puppet', 'Morning Glory' 2. The Sensational Alex Harvey Band 3. 'Bohemian Rhapsody' 4. Alvin Stardust 5. 'We Do It' 6. 'Baby Face' 7. Rachmaninoff ('Piano Concerto No. 2 in C minor') 8. 'Requiem' 9. Julie Covington (Devonia), Charlotte Cornwell (Anna), Rula Lenska (Nancy) 10. 'Love To Love You Baby'

1978

1. In March this year, who became the first woman in UK chart history to reach number one with a self-written song, and what was it called?

2. Which American teen idol of the late fifties and early sixties made a cameo appearance in the film *Grease* as 'Teen Angel'?

3. The number one soundtracks to *Saturday Night Fever* (18 consecutive weeks) and *Grease* (13 consecutive weeks) dominated the album charts in 1978. But between those two, the group that had the biggest selling single of the year held the number one album spot for a month. What is the name of the group? (Award yourself an extra point if you know the title of their number one album!)

4. The first Genesis single to reach the Top 10 was released in 1978. What was it called?

5. *Jeff Wayne's Musical Version of The War Of The Worlds* was one of the biggest selling albums of the year and featured a number of guest singers in the main roles. It included

Justin Hayward as the 'sung' thoughts of the Journalist. But which actor 'narrated' the role of the Journalist?

6 Earth, Wind & Fire reached the Top 40 with their version of which Lennon & McCartney song?

7 Which painter was the subject of Brian & Michael's number one 'Matchstalk Men and Matchstalk Cats and Dogs'?

8 *A Tonic For The Troops* was a hit album for The Boomtown Rats this year. Which of the band's singles has this title in its lyrics?

9 Under what name did the singer born Deirdre Cozier record her Top 5 hit 'Automatic Lover'?

10 What four words are heard at the very end of Electric Light Orchestra's 'Mr Blue Sky'?

ANSWERS TO 1977

1. Mary Hopkin 2. Graham Gouldman, Eric Stewart 3. 'Dancin' Easy' 4. Barry Blue 5. 'I Don't Want To Talk About It'/'First Cut Is The Deepest' by Rod Stewart 6. Supertramp 7. 'When I Need You' co-written with Albert Hammond 8. Billy & Bobby 9. Fifth Dimension 10. 'Another Funny Honeymoon'

1979

1. Having had a run of hits in the sixties with The Equals, Eddy Grant had his debut solo hit this year with which song?

2. Which Italian-born music producer co-wrote and produced the hit 'The Number One Song In Heaven' by Sparks?

3. American singer Linda Clifford had her only Top 40 hit in this year with a disco version of a number one from 1970. What is the song?

4. The Scottish band The Skids had their most successful chart year in 1979 with four Top 40 singles. But one member of the group would go on to have greater success in the eighties as lead singer and guitarist with Big Country. Who was he?

5. Prior to their Top 5 song 'Reunited' in the spring of 1979, the duo Peaches and Herb had reached the Top 40 for the first and only other time earlier in the year with the song 'Shake Your _____' what?

6. The songs 'Everybody's Happy Nowadays' and 'Harmony In My Head' were both hits in 1979 for which punk band?

7 The eighth and final studio album by Led Zeppelin was released this year. It reached number one in both the UK and the USA. What was it called?

8 The novelty hit 'Luton Airport' by Cats U.K. was inspired by a TV commercial for Campari starring which London-born actress?

9 B.A. Robertson made his chart debut in 1979 with the number two song 'Bang Bang'. He was held off number one by Cliff Richard's 'We Don't Talk Anymore'. But Robertson then had chart success in the early eighties as co-writer of two Top 5 singles for Cliff. Can you name either of them?

10 'He Was Beautiful', a vocal version of the theme music to *The Deer Hunter* was a Top 20 hit this year for which Welsh-born singer?

ANSWERS TO 1978

1. Kate Bush with 'Wuthering Heights' 2. Frankie Avalon 3. Boney M with *Nightflight To Venus* 4. 'Follow You Follow Me' 5. Richard Burton 6. 'Got To Get You Into My Life' 7. L.S.Lowry - the single officially had the subtitle '(Lowry's Song)' 8. 'She's So Modern' 9. Dee D. Jackson 10. 'Please turn me over' ('Mr Blue Sky' was a hit single in 1978 but was also the last song on side three of the group's double album *Out Of The Blue*.)

ABBA

1. What words follow in brackets on their 1979 Top 3 hit 'Gimme! Gimme! Gimme!'?
2. In 1972, Agnetha starred as Mary Magdalene in the Swedish production of which hit musical?
3. During the seventies, ABBA converted an unused cinema into a state-of-the-art recording studio in Stockholm. What did they name it?
4. Which 1981 Top 10 hit for the group was only released on 12-inch vinyl?
5. In 2021, ABBA returned to the Top 10 for the first time in 40 years with which song?

6 Which legendary singer and songwriter co-wrote their 1974 Top 40 hit 'Ring Ring'?

7 Written by Russ Ballard and produced by Phil Collins, Frida had a Top 20 American hit and pan-European Top 10 single in 1982–83 with which song?

8 To which organization did the group donate half of the royalties from their hit 'Chiquitita' in 1979?

9 Not counting their *Greatest Hits*, what is the title of their first number one album in the UK?

10 Benny and Björn collaborated with which successful lyricist to write the score for the musical *Chess*?

ANSWERS TO 1979

1. 'Living On The Front Line' 2. Giorgio Moroder 3. 'Bridge Over Troubled Water' 4. Stuart Adamson 5. 'Shake Your Groove Thing' 6. The Buzzcocks 7. *In Through The Out Door* 8. Lorraine Chase 9. 'Carrie' (No. 4 in 1980), 'Wired For Sound' (No. 4 in 1981) 10. Iris Williams

BLONDIE

1. An early version of the group's first number one, 'Heart Of Glass', had a different song title. What is that title?

2. Their UK chart debut 'Denis' had been an American Top 10 hit in 1963 under its original spelling 'Denise'. Which doo-wop group recorded it?

3. Blondie had only one original Top 40 hit in the noughties – it was Top 20 in 2003. What is it called?

4. Who was the band's keyboard player during the group's run of hits in the seventies and eighties, and rejoined the band for their chart comeback in the late nineties?

5. Released in 1979, what is the only hit single for the group that features a colour in its title?

6. Prior to Blondie, Debbie Harry had been in a folk-rock group in the late sixties that took

its name from the title of a book by Kenneth Grahame. What were they called?

7 The 1980 number one 'Call Me' was the theme for a hit film that year starring Richard Gere. What is the film?

8 Which acclaimed songwriter sang backing vocals on the songs 'Dreaming' and 'Atomic'?

9 Released in 1986, Clem Burke played drums on a Eurythmics album that included the singles 'Missionary Man', 'When Tomorrow Comes' and 'The Miracle Of Love'. What is the title of the album?

10 Who produced the group's albums *Parallel Lines*, *Eat To The Beat*, *Autoamerican* and *The Hunter*?

ANSWERS TO ABBA

1. '(A Man After Midnight)' 2. *Jesus Christ Superstar* 3. Polar Music Studio 4. 'Lay All Your Love On Me' 5. 'Don't Shut Me Down' 6. Neil Sedaka (Neil and collaborator Phil Cody provided the English lyrics for the song) 7. 'I Know There's Something Going On', the single stalled at No. 43 in UK) 8. UNICEF (ABBA increased royalties to 100% in 2014.) 9. *Arrival* (released 1976, No. 1 for a total of ten weeks in 1977) 10. Tim Rice

ELTON JOHN

1. What was the first Elton John single to top the American charts?

2. Which 1985 Top 3 hit by Elton featured backing vocals by George Michael with Nik Kershaw on guitar?

3. 'Live Like Horses' was a 1996 Top 10 duet with which classical singer?

4. Elton's first solo single appeared on the Philips record label in 1968. What was its title?

5. What is Elton's adopted middle name?

6 Under what pseudonyms did Bernie Taupin and Elton write 'Don't Go Breaking My Heart'?

7 In 1969, Elton and Bernie Taupin wrote a song for Lulu to perform in the heats to choose the UK's entry for the Eurovision Song Contest. What was its title?

8 Which of Elton's singles in the early eighties was recorded as a tribute to John Lennon?

9 What was the title of Ladbaby's 2021 number one that featured Ed Sheeran and Elton?

10 What was the name of the band Elton helped form in the sixties, in which Long John Baldry was the lead singer?

ANSWERS TO BLONDIE

1. 'Once I Had A Love (aka The Disco Song)' 2. Randy & The Rainbows 3. 'Good Boys' 4. Jimmy Destri 5. 'Union City Blue' 6. The Wind in the Willows 7. *American Gigolo* 8. Ellie Greenwich 9. *Revenge* 10. Mike Chapman

HOT CHOCOLATE

1. What was the title of Hot Chocolate's first Top 10 hit?

2. Which member of the group released a single in 1969 on the Bell label titled 'Baby I Love, Love I Love You'?

3. In 1987, Errol Brown achieved his only solo Top 40 hit. What was the title?

4. Who supplied the deep, disgruntled spoken voice on their 1973 Top 10 single 'Brother Louie'?

5. Although different songs, which 1983 Top 40 entry for the group shares its title with the 1976 Top 40 and only UK hit by Claude François?

6. Which major Hot Chocolate hit began life as the B-side to 'Blue Night', one of the group's very few non-charting singles in the seventies?

7 'Lady Barbara', an Italian song adapted into English by Errol Brown and Tony Wilson, reached the Top 20 in 1970 for which chart act?

8 Apart from re-issues, what was the title of the group's final Top 10 single?

9 Their 1978 hit 'I'll Put You Together Again' was written by Don Black and Geoff Stephens for which proposed stage musical?

10 Which Dutch record producer and DJ was responsible for the 1987 remixes of 'You Sexy Thing' and 'Every 1's A Winner'?

ANSWERS TO ELTON JOHN

1. 'Crocodile Rock' 2. 'Nikita' 3. Luciano Pavarotti 4. 'I've Been Loving You' 5. Hercules 6. Ann Orson and Carte Blanche 7. 'I Can't Go On Living Without You' 8. 'Empty Garden (Hey Hey Johnny)' (Top 20 in America, but stalled at No. 51 in UK) 9. 'Sausage Rolls For Everyone' 10. Bluesology

QUEEN

1 *Sheer Heart Attack* is the title of the group's 1974 album. But which of their studio albums includes a song with that same title?

2 The video for 'Radio Ga Ga' included scenes from a 1920s German film. What is that film? (And for two bonus points, can you name the directors of both the video and the German film?)

3 'I Can Hear Music', a song that had been recorded in the sixties by both The Ronettes and The Beach Boys, was sung by Freddie Mercury on a 1973 single. Under what pseudonym was it released?

4 Which song, originally a hit for the group in 1980, returned to the charts in 1998 as a Top 5 remix billed as Queen and Wyclef Jean featuring Pras and Free, then again as a different Top 40 remix in 2006 billed as Queen vs The Miami Project?

5 What was the first hit A-side to be written by bass player John Deacon?

6 Part of the closing track on the 1976 album *A Day At The Races* is not sung in English. Which other language features on this closing song?

7 Shakin' Stevens, billed as 'Shaky', reached the Top 40 in 1992 with the song 'Radio'. Which member of Queen was billed alongside him on the single?

8 The words 'Fried Chicken' are heard at the end of which 1985 Top 10 hit?

9 What is the name of the group Brian May formed in the late sixties and which Roger Taylor joined as drummer?

10 Queen performed a critically acclaimed set at Live Aid, but later in the evening Freddie Mercury and Brian May returned to the stage to perform the poignant closing song from the album *The Works*. What is the song called?

ANSWERS TO HOT CHOCOLATE

1. 'Love Is Life' 2. Tony Wilson 3. 'Personal Touch' 4. Alexis Korner 5. 'Tears On The Telephone' 6. 'You Sexy Thing' 7. Peter Noone & Herman's Hermits 8. 'What Kind Of Boy You Looking For (Girl)' 9. *Dear Anyone* 10. Ben Liebrand

1980s GOLDEN YEARS

Leg warmers, slogan T-shirts, shoulder pads, power suits vs shell suits! *Bananaman, Danger Mouse, Beat the Teacher, Saturday Superstore* and *Jossy's Giants.*

1980s POPMASTER 1

1. In 1982, Dionne Warwick made a chart comeback with which Top 3 song written by The Gibb Brothers?

2. What are the first names of the two Kane brothers who, as Hue and Cry, had a Top 10 hit with 'Labour of Love' in 1987?

3. Which group had Top 10 singles in the mid-eighties called 'Love And Pride' and 'Alone Without You' and Top 40 hits with 'Won't You Hold My Hand Now' and 'The Taste Of Your Tears'?

4. Which 1984 Top 10 single by Billy Ocean has the subtitle '(No More Love On The Run)'?

5. The titles of three Top 10 singles by Odyssey in the early eighties end with the word 'Out'. The number one 'Use It Up And Wear It Out' is one of them. What are the other two?

6 Released in 1980 and 1989, which singer's first and last Top 40 hits of the eighties were called 'Looking For Clues' and 'Change His Ways'?

7 Neneh Cherry made her chart debut in 1988 with which song?

8 Which group was 'Calling All The Heroes' according to the title of their 1986 Top 10 single?

9 The singer Pat Benatar had three Top 40 songs during the eighties. Can you name one of them?

10 The songs 'Sunset Now' and 'This Is Mine' were Top 40 singles in 1984 for which group?

ANSWERS TO QUEEN

1. *News Of The World* (1977) 2. *Metropolis* (David Mallet directed the video for 'Radio Ga Ga' and *Metropolis* was directed by Fritz Lang.) 3. Larry Lurex 4. 'Another One Bites The Dust' 5. 'You're My Best Friend' (No. 7 in 1976) 6. Japanese (The song is 'Teo Torriate (Let Us Cling Together)') 7. Roger Taylor (Billed as Shaky featuring Roger Taylor) 8. 'One Vision' 9. Smile 10. 'Is This The World We Created...?'

1980s POPMASTER 2

1. In 1984, George Michael reached number one with the song 'Careless _____' what?

2. Which group had a hit in 1989 with the song 'Woman In Chains' and which singer joined them on the track?

3. What '_____ Street' did Prince sing about in the title of his 1988 Top 10 single?

4. Four of Kim Wilde's Top 40 hits in the eighties include the word 'Love' in the title. 'Chequered Love' was the first. Can you name one of the other three?

5. Which vocalist featured on Mike Oldfield's 1983 Top 10 single 'Moonlight Shadow'?

6 Erasure made their Top 40 debut in 1986 with which Top 3 song?

7 Which French-based group had their only Top 40 hit in 1989 with a Top 5 song about a Brazilian dance called 'Lambada'?

8 The group Whitesnake had both of their Top 10 singles in 1987. Can you name them?

9 The 1986 Top 3 single 'My Favourite Waste Of Time' was the only Top 40 hit for which singer?

10 The songs 'Slow Hand', 'Automatic' and 'I'm So Excited' were all hits in the eighties for which American family group?

ANSWERS TO 1980s POPMASTER 1

1. 'Heartbreaker' 2. Pat & Greg Kane 3. King 4. 'Caribbean Queen (No More Love On The Run)' 5. 'If You're Looking For A Way Out' (No. 6 in 1980), 'Inside Out' (No. 3 in 1982) 6. Robert Palmer 7. 'Buffalo Stance' (entered Top 40 in December 1988, peaked at No. 3 early 1989) 8. It Bites 9. 'We Belong', 'Love Is A Battlefield', All Fired Up' 10. Heaven 17

1980s POPMASTER 3

1 Which duo reached number one in 1987 with the song 'It's A Sin'?

2 Four of Alison Moyet's Top 40 hits in the eighties have the word 'Love' somewhere in the title, her debut 'Love Resurrection' and the Top 3 single 'That Ole Devil Called Love' are two of them. Can you name the other two?

3 Which group's hit singles in the first half of the eighties included 'A Lover's Holiday', 'Searching' and 'Change Of Heart'?

4 Prefab Sprout had their only Top 10 single in 1988 with which song?

5 Which duo made their chart debut in 1986 with the song 'Showing Out (Get Fresh at The Weekend)'?

6 A cover of which Elvis Presley hit gave Fine Young Cannibals a Top 10 single in 1986?

7 The song 'Tunnel of Love' reached the Top 10 in 1983 for which group?

8 David Grant and Jaki Graham had two hit duets in 1985. Can you name either of them?

9 'Missing You' was a 1984 Top 10 hit for a singer who had previously been in a group called The Babys and would go on to be a member of Anglo/American rock band Bad English. Who is he?

10 Ray Parker Jr is best known for his 1984 Top 3 single 'Ghostbusters', but he did have one other Top 40 hit in the eighties which reached the Top 20 in 1987. What is its title?

ANSWERS TO 1980s POPMASTER 2

1. 'Careless Whisper' 2. Tears For Fears, Oleta Adams 3. 'Alphabet Street' 4. 'Love Blonde' (No. 23 in 1983), 'Rage To Love' (No. 19 in 1985), 'Love In A Natural Way' (No. 32 in 1989) (Her Top 40 hit 'Love Is Holy' was in the nineties.) 5. Maggie Reilly 6. 'Sometimes' (The song 'Oh L'Amour', which was released before this, only became a Top 40 hit when it was remixed in 2003.) 7. Kaoma 8. 'Is This Love', 'Here I Go Again' (both reached No. 9) 9. Owen Paul 10. The Pointer Sisters

1980s POPMASTER 4

1. Who reached number one in 1982 with the song 'Goody Two Shoes'?

2. What was the title of Matt Bianco's Top 40 debut in 1984?

3. The American singer who had a Top 5 single in 1980 with 'Never Knew Love Like This Before' is called Stephanie _____ what?

4. Alexander O'Neal had a Top 10 duet in the mid-eighties with Cherrelle on the song 'Saturday Love'. But what is his only solo single to reach the Top 10 during the decade?

5. Tracy Tracy is the name of the lead singer with the group that had a Top 5 hit with 'Crash' in 1988. What is the name of the group?

6 What 'Sister _____' did Thompson Twins sing about on the group's 1984 Top 20 single?

7 The 1982 hit 'Trouble' was the only solo Top 40 hit for a member of Fleetwood Mac at the time. Can you name which one?

8 The songs 'Like To Get To Know You Well' and 'Look Mama' both reached the Top 10 in the mid-eighties for which singer and keyboard player?

9 Bobby Brown's Top 5 song 'On Our Own' featured on the soundtrack to one of 1989's most anticipated sequels. What is the film?

10 The duo Boy Meets Girl had their only Top 40 hit in the late eighties with which Top 10 song?

ANSWERS TO 1980s POPMASTER 3

1. Pet Shop Boys 2. 'Is This Love?' and 'Love Letters' (both Top 5 singles) 3. Change 4. 'The King Of Rock N' Roll' 5. Mel & Kim 6. 'Suspicious Minds' 7. Fun Boy Three 8. 'Could It Be I'm Falling In Love' (No. 5), 'Mated' (No. 20) 9. John Waite 10. 'I Don't Think That Man Should Sleep Alone'

1980s POPMASTER 5

1. The lead singer of Led Zeppelin had a solo hit in 1983 with 'Big Log'. Who is he?

2. 1983's 'True' is one of six Top 40 songs by Spandau Ballet to have a one-word title. How many of the other five can you name?

3. The songs 'Breathing' in 1980 and 'This Woman's Work' in 1989 were the first and last Top 40 hits of the eighties for which artist?

4. Van Halen had two Top 10 singles during the eighties. 'Jump' was one, what is the other one called?

5. Who made her chart debut in 1985 with the Top 10 song 'Say I'm Your Number One'?

6 Which song gave the singer and pianist Nina Simone a Top 5 single in 1987?

7 D-Mob featuring Gary Haisman had a Top 3 hit in 1988 with 'We Call It _____' what?

8 'This Is Me', 'I Won't Bleed For You' and 'Love Like A River' were all Top 40 hits in the late eighties for which duo?

9 Which group reached the Top 20 in 1983 with a cover of the Jimmy Cliff song 'Many Rivers To Cross'?

10 Which Top 10 song by Scritti Politti has the subtitle '(Pray Like Aretha Franklin)'?

ANSWERS TO 1980s POPMASTER 4

1. Adam Ant 2. 'Get Out Of Your Lazy Bed' 3. Stephanie Mills 4. 'Criticize' (No. 4 in 1987) 5. The Primitives 6. 'Sister Of Mercy' 7. Lindsey Buckingham 8. Howard Jones 9. *Ghostbusters II* 10. 'Waiting For A Star To Fall'

1980s POPMASTER 6

1. The duo that had a Top 3 single in 1986 with 'Let's Go All The Way' was called Sly _____ what?

2. What was the title of the first solo Top 20 hit achieved by Nick Heyward?

3. From 1983, can you name the group who said 'Don't Stop That Crazy Rhythm'?

4. Which song is listed alongside 'Push It' on Salt-N'-Pepa's 1988 Top 3 hit?

5. Which legendary guitarist was featured on the 1986 Top 10 instrumental 'Peter Gunn' by The Art of Noise?

6. What was the title of the only single by The Moody Blues to make the Top 40 during the eighties?

7 Which of these three hits by Orchestral Manoeuvres in the Dark gained the highest chart position? Was it 'Talking Loud And Clear', 'Locomotion' or '(Forever) Live And Die'?

8 The hit singles 'Brilliant Disguise' and 'Tougher Than The Rest' featured on which 1987 album by Bruce Springsteen?

9 Can you name the female singer who made the Top 5 in 1989 with her version of Maxine Nightingale's 1975 hit 'Right Back Where We Started From'?

10 Which act had a number one album in 1983 called *You and Me Both*?

ANSWERS TO 1980s POPMASTER 5

1. Robert Plant 2. 'Gold', 'Communication' (both 1983), 'Lifeline', 'Instinction' (both 1982), 'Glow' (a double A-side with 'Muscle Bound' in 1981) (Their 1988 single 'Raw' failed to reach the Top 40.) 3. Kate Bush 4. 'Why Can't This Be Love' 5. Princess 6. 'My Baby Just Cares For Me' (Previously released in 1985 but failed to make Top 40.) 7. 'We Call It Acieed' 8. Climie Fisher 9. UB40 10. 'Wood Beez (Pray Like Aretha Franklin)'

1980s POPMASTER 7

1. Who topped the charts in 1988 with 'Nothing's Gonna Change My Love For You'?

2. What was the title of the first Top 20 hit for Shakin' Stevens?

3. What four words in brackets follow the title of Billy Ocean's 1986 hit 'There'll Be Sad Songs'?

4. Who had a Top 20 single in 1988 with a song called 'Monkey'?

5. Which rock band made the Top 3 in the late eighties with 'Can I Play With Madness'?

6 Which of these three hits by Cliff Richard gained the highest chart position? Was it 'The Best Of Me', 'The Only Way Out' or 'Little Town'?

7 Can you name the chart act that had a number one album in 1987 with *Keep Your Distance*?

8 Which group reached the Top 10 in 1984 with their version of Dion's hit 'The Wanderer'?

9 What was the title of Rod Stewart's only number one single during the eighties?

10 Who is the Spanish guitarist who had a Top 10 hit in 1984 with 'Love Theme From *The Thorn Birds*'?

ANSWERS TO 1980s POPMASTER 6

1. Sly Fox 2. 'Whistle Down The Wind' 3. Modern Romance 4. 'Tramp' 5. Duane Eddy 6. 'Blue World' 7. 'Locomotion' (Reached No. 5 in '84 - the other two both peaked at No. 11.) 8. *Tunnel Of Love* 9. Sinitta 10. Yazoo

1980s POPMASTER 8

1. Madonna's chart debut reached number six in 1984 and then number two when it re-entered the charts the following year. What is its one-word title?

2. In 1986, Patti Labelle made the Top 3 with the duet 'On My Own', which she recorded with which male vocalist?

3. The Fureys with Davey Arthur had their one and only Top 20 hit in 1981. What is the title of the song?

4. From 1989, can you name the act whose 'Do The Right Thing' was the only major hit they achieved?

5. Complete the title of this 1982 Top 3 song by Kid Creole & The Coconuts: 'Annie, I'm Not ____' what?

6 Originally both a Top 10 hit for The Jacksons and Top 20 for the song's co-writer Mick Jackson in 1978, which act took the song 'Blame It On The Boogie' into the Top 5 in 1989?

7 Released in 1988, can you name the successful rap and hip-hop group that was featured on Samantha Fox's hit 'Naughty Girls (Need Love Too)'?

8 Bon Jovi reached the Top 20 for the first time in 1986 with which song?

9 'Wild World' was a Top 5 hit in the late eighties for Maxi Priest. Who wrote the song?

10 What was the title of the only Top 40 single for Suzi Quatro during the eighties?

ANSWERS TO 1980s POPMASTER 7

1. Glenn Medeiros 2. 'Marie Marie' 3. 'There'll Be Sad Songs (To Make You Cry)' 4. George Michael 5. Iron Maiden 6. 'The Best Of Me' (Reached No. 2 in 1989, 'The Only Way Out' No. 10 and 'Little Town' No. 11, both in 1982.) 7. Curiosity Killed The Cat 8. Status Quo 9. 'Baby Jane' (No. 1 for three weeks in 1983) 10. Juan Martin

1980s POPMASTER 9

1. Joe Cocker and Jennifer Warnes had a Top 10 duet in 1983 with a song taken from the film *An Officer and a Gentleman*. What is it called?

2. 'Circus Games' was a Top 40 hit in 1980 for which Scottish band?

3. Billy Idol reached the Top 10 in 1987 with a cover of which number one by Tommy James and the Shondells?

4. Who wrote Martika's 1989 hit 'I Feel The Earth Move'?

5. Can you name the group whose debut album *Picture Book* reached the Top 3 in the mid-eighties?

6 Bruce Hornsby and the Range had their only Top 40 hit in 1986 with a song that was also an American number one. What is it called?

7 What was the title of the first hit by T'Pau, which reached the Top 5 in 1987?

8 The 1983 song 'Don't Talk To Me About Love' was the third and final Top 10 single for which group?

9 In the late eighties, 'Don't Worry Be Happy' was a hit single for Bobby ____ who?

10 Talking Heads first reached the Top 40 in 1981 with which Top 20 song?

ANSWERS TO 1980s POPMASTER 8

1. 'Holiday' 2. Michael McDonald 3. 'When You Were Sweet Sixteen' 4. Redhead Kingpin and the FBI 5. 'Annie, I'm Not Your Daddy' 6. Big Fun 7. Full Force 8. 'You Give Love A Bad Name' 9. Cat Stevens 10. 'Mama's Boy'

1980s POPMASTER 10

1. Toyah's chart debut came in 1981 with the Top 5 EP, *Four From Toyah*. The lead song on it was called 'It's A _____' what?

2. Sharpe And Numan had a Top 20 hit in 1985 with 'Change Your Mind', but do you know their first names?

3. Featuring Jim Diamond on vocals, which chart act had a Top 3 single in 1982 called 'I Won't Let You Down'?

4. The only hit for Minneapolis band Lipps Inc reached the Top 3 in 1980. What was it called?

5. According to her 1986 Top 5 single, who said there 'Ain't Nothin' Goin' On But The Rent'?

6 In 1988, Bros had a Top 3 double A-side with 'Cat Among The Pigeons' and which other song?

7 What was the title of the 1984 chart debut by Cyndi Lauper?

8 Can you name the American rock band that made its Top 10 album chart debut in 1989 with *Doolittle*?

9 Which chart act had Top 20 singles in 1985 called 'Lost Weekend' and 'Brand New Friend'?

10 What four words in brackets complete the title of Wham!'s 1983 hit, 'Wham Rap!'?

ANSWERS TO 1980s POPMASTER 9

1. 'Up Where We Belong' 2. The Skids 3. 'Mony Mony' 4. Carole King 5. Simply Red 6. 'The Way It Is' 7. 'Heart And Soul' 8. Altered Images 9. Bobby McFerrin 10. 'Once In A Lifetime'

1980

1. R.E.M. played their first ever gig this year, in a converted Episcopalian church in the city where they formed. What is the name of that city?

2. Olivia Newton-John and Electric Light Orchestra reached number one with 'Xanadu' from the film with the same name. But Electric Light Orchestra had three other hit singles in 1980 that all featured on the soundtrack. Can you name one of them? (Or give yourself three points if you can name all three!)

3. Neil Diamond starred alongside Sir Laurence Olivier in a musical drama and released an accompanying soundtrack album this year. What is the title of the film and album?

4. Which British singer and rapper, born this year, had a Top 20 hit in 2004 called '1980', in which she sang and rapped about her childhood years?

5. In the video for which song did Paul McCartney impersonate Ron Mael of Sparks, an early Beatles version of himself, Hank Marvin and a drummer loosely based on John Bonham of Led Zeppelin?

6 Although it failed to reach the charts, light entertainment group The Barron Knights released a single set to the music of Gary Numan's 'Cars' called 'We Know Who Done It (Pt 1) (Cars)'. The song was about which television 'event'?

7 Kelly Marie had a number one this year with 'Feels Like I'm In Love'. Who wrote the song?

8 Which group first reached the Top 40 with the single 'C'30, C'60. C'90 Go'?

9 UB40 released their Top 3 debut album this year. Its title was effectively the opposite of the group's name. What was it called?

10 Having had two hit singles the previous year, which group made their final Top 40 appearance in 1980 with the Top 20 song 'My World'?

ANSWERS TO 1980s POPMASTER 10

1. 'It's A Mystery' 2. Bill (Sharpe) and Gary (Numan) 3. PhD 4. 'Funkytown' 5. Gwen Guthrie 6. 'Silent Night' 7. 'Girls Just Want To Have Fun' 8. Pixies (*Doolittle* was the band's second album; the first, *Surfer Rosa*, failed to chart in the UK.) 9. Lloyd Cole and the Commotions 10. 'Wham Rap! (Enjoy What You Do)'

1981

1. What is the subtitle of Haircut 100's debut hit 'Favourite Shirts'?

2. Who played the fairy godmother in the video to the Adam and the Ants song 'Prince Charming'?

3. Written by Rod Temperton and taken from the album *The Dude*, 'Razzamatazz' was a Top 20 hit for Quincy Jones. But who sang lead vocals on the track, and also provided backing vocals for the album's other big hit 'Ai No Corrida'?

4. The duo Godley & Creme had two Top 10 singles this year. Can you name either of them?

5. Which singer joined Iron Maiden in 1981 as the band's lead vocalist?

6. *Face Value*, the number one debut solo album by Phil Collins, contained three hit singles this year: 'In The Air Tonight', 'I Missed Again' and which other song?

7 Keith Marshall had a solo hit with the song 'Only Crying'. But this wasn't his first time in the charts. He'd reached the Top 10 twice in the mid-seventies as guitarist with which band?

8 American act Hi-Gloss made its one and only UK chart appearance in 1981 with which Top 20 single?

9 The Eurovision-winning line-up of Bucks Fizz consisted of Jay Aston, Cheryl Baker, Mike Nolan and which other singer?

10 'Vienna' by Ultravox was famously kept from being number one by 'Shaddap You Face' by Joe Dolce Music Theatre. But it was also stopped from reaching number one by one other song. What is that song and who recorded it?

ANSWERS TO 1980

1. Athens, Georgia 2. 'I'm Alive', 'All Over The World', 'Don't Walk Away' 3. *The Jazz Singer* 4. Estelle 5. 'Coming Up' 6. 'Who Shot J.R.?' (*Dallas*) 7. Ray Dorset (of Mungo Jerry) 8. Bow Wow Wow 9. *Signing Off* 10. Secret Affair

1982

1. 'Beat Surrender' was number one for The Jam in the month the group split up. What were the names of Paul Weller's two bandmates?

2. Trevor Horn produced ABC's *The Lexicon Of Love*, one of the bestselling albums of 1982. The group wanted to work with him having heard his production of which 1981 hit single?

3. The singer Charlene was a one-hit wonder when her single 'I've Never Been To Me' reached number one in June this year. On what record label was it released?

4. Directed by Alan Parker, a film version of Pink Floyd's *The Wall* premiered at the Cannes Film Festival this year. Which singer played the lead role of Pink?

5. The Emerald Express is billed alongside which group on which number one?

6. The England World Cup Squad had a Top 3 hit this year with 'This Time (We'll Get It Right)' written by Chris Norman and Pete Spencer, who'd had a run of hits in the seventies as members of which band?

7 Born Jacques Pépino, under what name did this singer have a Top 10 hit called 'Saddle Up'?

8 With over fifty Top 40 appearances, Queen is one of the most successful singles acts in the UK. But in this year they released their least performing Top 40 single, spending one week in the Top 40 at number 40. What is it called?

9 Released in the summer of 1982, *Love And Dancing* is the title of one of the earliest remix albums. It featured remixes of tracks from *Dare* by the Human League as well as a former B-side called 'Hard Times'. Under what name did the group release this Top 3 remix album?

10 Toni Basil's hit 'Mickey' had previously been recorded under its original title by the band Racey as a track on their 1979 album *Smash And Grab*. What was that original title?

ANSWERS TO 1981

1. 'Favourite Shirts (Boy Meets Girl)' 2. Diana Dors 3. Patti Austin 4. 'Under Your Thumb' (No. 3), 'Wedding Bells' (No. 7) 5. Bruce Dickinson 6. 'If Leaving Me Is Easy' 7. Hello 8. 'You'll Never Know' 9. Bobby G/Bobby Gee 10. 'Woman', by John Lennon (Ultravox spent four weeks at No. 2, the first of which was because of this song.)

1983

1. 'The Chinese Way' is the title of a Top 30 hit for which group?

2. Who duetted with Kenny Rogers on the song 'We've Got Tonight'?

3. The debut number one album by Tears For Fears was released this year and included the singles 'Mad World', 'Change' and 'Pale Shelter'. What is it called?

4. 'Bad Day' was the title of the 1983 Top 20 debut by which chart act?

5. Mark Knopfler provided the soundtrack to a Scottish comedy drama starring Burt Lancaster, Peter Riegert, Denis Lawson and Fulton Mackay. What is the title of the film?

6. Which chart act sang 'There's Something Wrong In Paradise' this year?

7 Beginning with the earliest, put these four songs in the order they were number one this year: 'Candy Girl' by New Edition, 'Down Under' by Men At Work, 'Only You' by The Flying Pickets and 'Give It Up' by KC and the Sunshine Band?

8 Released in 1983, 'Love On Your Side', the first Top 40 hit for Thompson Twins, includes a musical reference to a single the group released the previous year, but failed to chart. What is that single?

9 Can you name the band that made both of their Top 40 appearances in this year with the singles 'Dream To Sleep' and 'Just Outside Of Heaven'?

10 Which group followed up their 1983 Top 3 hit 'I.O.U.' with a Top 30 single called 'Pop Goes My Love'?

ANSWERS TO 1982

1. Bruce Foxton, Rick Buckler 2. 'Hand Held In Black And White' by Dollar 3. Motown 4. Bob Geldof 5. 'Come On Eileen' by Dexy's Midnight Runners & The Emerald Express 6. Smokie 7. David Christie 8. 'Backchat' 9. The League Unlimited Orchestra (an affectionate play on Barry White's Love Unlimited Orchestra) 10. 'Kitty'

1984

1. *The Unforgettable Fire* was a number one album this year for which group?

2. The actor Nigel Planer had a Top 3 version of Traffic's 'Hole In My Shoe' this year, which he recorded as his character from a BBC TV comedy. What was the comedy called and what was the name of his character?

3. What is the title of the Top 20 single by The Jacksons that features Mick Jagger as guest vocalist?

4. The duo Blancmange reached the charts this year with a cover of ABBA's 'The Day Before You Came', but they made a slight change to the lyrics. Neil Arthur substituted the name of feminist author Marilyn French for which writer?

5. 1984 saw the group Re-Flex have the only Top 40 hit of their chart career. What was the title of this song?

6 Martin Brammer has co-written hits for Lighthouse Family, Rachel Stevens, Olly Murs and James Morrison. But his original chart success was as lead singer on the hits 'Closest Thing To Heaven' and 'Respect Yourself' with which group?

7 Terri Wells had her only UK Top 40 single with her version of a 1972 American Top 3 hit for The Detroit Spinners. What is the song?

8 Which group's two-year Top 40 career ended this year with the song 'The More You Live, The More You Love'?

9 'Let's Hear It For The Boy' was a Top 3 hit for Deniece Williams. It featured on the soundtrack to which film starring Kevin Bacon?

10 Which duo first reached the Top 40 this year with 'Each And Everyone'?

ANSWERS TO 1983

1. Level 42 2. Sheena Easton 3. *The Hurting* 4. Carmel (Carmel was the name of both the lead singer and the group) 5. *Local Hero* 6. Kid Creole and the Coconuts 7. 'Down Under' (January), 'Candy Girl' (May), 'Give It Up' (August), 'Only You' (December) 8. 'In The Name Of Love' 9. H2O (a different chart act also called H2O had dance hits in the nineties) 10. Freeez

1985

1. What was going to be the original title of Kate Bush's song 'Running Up That Hill'?

2. German band Propaganda had a hit with 'Duel' this year. Who was the lead singer on the track?

3. Which singer joined Bronski Beat on a Top 10 medley of 'Love To Love You Baby', 'I Feel Love' and 'Johnny Remember Me'?

4. The song 'I Know Him So Well' by Elaine Paige and Barbara Dickson was taken from which stage musical?

5. The Top 5 song 'Feel So Real' and the Top 40 single 'Dancin' In The Key Of Life' were the only two UK chart appearances by Steve _____ who?

6. What 1985 number one shares its title with a different song that had been number one the previous year? (Bonus point if you can name both chart acts as well!)

7 Which boy soprano is billed alongside Sarah Brightman on the Top 3 single 'Pie Jesu'?

8 In 1985, which chart act was widely reported as being the first Western pop group to visit China?

9 British R&B act Loose Ends had their first Top 40 single this year with a song subtitled '(Contemplating)'. What is its full title?

10 'The Man's Too Strong', 'Why Worry' and 'Ride Across The River' are three of the tracks on the UK's biggest selling album of the year. What is it called and who recorded it?

ANSWERS TO 1984

1. U2 (The title track was a Top 10 single the following year.) 2. *The Young Ones*, Neil 3. 'State Of Shock' 4. Barbara Cartland 5. 'The Politics Of Dancing' 6. The Kane Gang 7. 'I'll Be Around' (The Detroit Spinners known just as The Spinners in America.) 8. A Flock Of Seagulls 9. *Footloose* 10. Everything But The Girl

1986

1. The Police had a Top 40 hit this year with a new version of one of their number one singles: which one?

2. Who became the youngest-ever winner of the Eurovision Song Contest with the Belgian entry *'J'aime La Vie'*?

3. Which actress had a Top 3 single called 'Starting Together' and for what BBC TV reality series was it the theme song?

4. What was the title of Boris Gardiner's Top 20 follow-up to his number one 'I Want To Wake Up With You'?

5. Which film featured Sade as Athene Duncannon, Ray Davies of The Kinks as Arthur, Sandie Shaw as Baby Boom's Mother, DJ Alan Freeman as Call-Me-Cobber and Bruno Tonioli as a Maltese Lodger?

6 This year's single 'God Thank You Woman' ended a run of ten Top 40 hits in the eighties for which group?

7 The lead singer with Arctic Monkeys and The Last Shadow Puppets was born this year. Who is he?

8 The lead singer and founder of The Mighty Wah! had his only solo Top 40 hit of the decade in 1986. Who is he and what is the title of the song?

9 'Shellshock' and 'State Of The Nation' were both hits for which group?

10 In the mid-eighties, 'Amityville (The House On The Hill)' became a Top 20 single and only Top 40 hit for which American rapper?

ANSWERS TO 1985

1. 'A Deal With God' 2. Claudia Brücken 3. Marc Almond 4. Chess 5. Steve Arrington 6. 'The Power Of Love' (Jennifer Rush in 1985, Frankie Goes To Hollywood in 1984) 7. Paul Miles-Kingston 8. Wham! 9. 'Hangin' On A String (Contemplating)' 10. *Brothers In Arms* by Dire Straits

1987

1 'Got My Mind Set On You' was a Top 3 hit this year for which former Beatle?

2 Johnny Logan won the Eurovision Song Contest for the second time this year with 'Hold Me Now'. But he'd go on and win it for a third time five years later as the writer of Linda Martin's Irish entry. What was this called?

3 The songs 'Wonderful Life' and 'Sweetest Smile' were both Top 10 this year for the singer Black. What was his real name?

4 Which multi-platinum album by Fleetwood Mac included the songs 'Big Love', 'Seven Wonders', 'Little Lies' and 'Family Man'?

5 Eric Clapton's hit 'Behind The Mask' is a cover of a song originally recorded by which Japanese group?

6 Beginning with the earliest, put these four songs in the order they were number one this year: 'Who's That Girl' by Madonna, 'Everything I Own' by Boy George, 'You Win Again' by The

Bee Gees and 'Nothing's Gonna Stop Us Now' by Starship?

7 Wax had a Top 20 hit with the song 'Bridge To Your Heart'. 10cc's Graham Gouldman was one half of the duo. Who was the other member?

8 The James Bond film *The Living Daylights* was released in 1987. a-ha provided the opening theme song, but which group recorded 'If There Was A Man', the song heard over the closing credits?

9 The duo Scarlet Fantastic made their only Top 40 appearance this year with which song?

10 Which chart act had its highest charting single of the decade with the Top 10 song 'April Skies'?

ANSWERS TO 1986

1. 'Don't Stand So Close To Me' (titled 'Don't Stand So Close To Me '86) 2. Sandra Kim (13 years old) 3. Su Pollard - BBC TV series called *The Marriage* 4. 'You're Everything To Me' (peaked at No. 11) 5. *Absolute Beginners* 6. Culture Club (The group reformed and had further hits in the late nineties.) 7. Alex Turner 8. Pete Wylie - 'Sinful' 9. New Order 10. Lovebug Starski

1988

1. Which number one song from this year had featured in an advert for a popular soft drink?

2. Along with Luke & Matt Goss, who was the third member of Bros when the group reached number one with 'I Owe You Nothing'?

3. The songs 'Talkin' Bout A Revolution', 'Baby Can I Hold You' and 'For You' all featured on the multi-million selling debut album by which singer-songwriter?

4. Dieter Meier and Boris Blank are the two members of a Swiss act that reached the Top 10 with 'The Race'. What is the name of the act?

5. Taken from the 1988 album *The Sea Of Love*, which Belfast band made their only Top 40 appearance with the Top 20 song 'Broken Land'?

6. A Tribe of Toffs had a Christmas novelty hit this year with which single?

7 'Soldier Of Love' was the only Top 40 hit of the eighties for a teen pin-up from the seventies. Who is he?

8 Fairground Attraction reached number one with 'Perfect', but what is the title of the group's Top 10 follow-up?

9 What are the first names of Stock Aitken Waterman, whose run of hits with Kylie Minogue began this year?

10 U2's *Rattle And Hum* was a number one album around the world in 1988 and included four UK Top 10 singles in the late eighties. The number one 'Desire' was the first, can you name the other three? (And award yourself an extra point if you get them in the order of release!)

ANSWERS TO 1987

1. George Harrison 2. 'Why Me?' 3. Colin Vearncombe 4. *Tango In The Night* 5. Yellow Magic Orchestra 6. 'Everything I Own' (March), 'Nothing's Gonna Stop Us Now' (May), 'Who's That Girl' (July), 'You Win Again' (October) 7. Andrew Gold 8. The Pretenders (Released as a single as 'The Pretenders for 007', it reached No. 49.) 9. 'No Memory' (*but if you did remember, give yourself an extra point!*) 10. The Jesus And Mary Chain (No. 8 - the band had one other Top 10 single, 'Reverence', which was No. 10 in 1992.)

1989

1. Simply Red reached the Top 3 this year with a song that had been a hit for Harold Melvin & the Bluenotes. What is the song?

2. Who co-wrote, co-produced and duetted with Madonna on 'Love Song', a track on her number one album *Like A Prayer*?

3. Liza Minnelli had a hit with a song from the Stephen Sondheim musical *Follies*. Produced by Pet Shop Boys, what is it called?

4. Which singer was the featured vocalist on the Soul II Soul hits 'Keep On Movin' and 'Back To Life (However Do You Want Me)'?

5. Edie Brickell and the New Bohemians made their debut Top 40 appearance this year with a song that would be a Top 3 cover ten years later. What is the song? (And a bonus point if you know who recorded the hit cover version!)

6. Who is the first male singer to be heard on the Band Aid II version of 'Do They Know It's Christmas?'?

7 Debbie Harry had a Top 20 single this year called 'I Want That Man'. It was written by members of which successful chart act of the eighties?

8 'Swing The Mood' was the first of three number ones for Jive Bunny and the Mastermixers. Can you name one of the other two?

9 Kirsty MacColl reached the Top 20 this year with her version of a song that had been a Top 20 single for The Kinks in 1968. What is the song?

10 The songs 'Hey Music Lover' and 'Mantra For A State Of Mind' were hits in 1989 for which chart act?

ANSWERS TO 1988

1. 'First Time' by Robin Beck 2. Craig Logan 3. *Tracy Chapman* by Tracy Chapman 4. Yello 5. The Adventures 6. 'John Kettley (Is A Weatherman)' 7. Donny Osmond 8. 'Find My Love' 9. Mike Stock, Matt Aitken, Pete Waterman 10. 'Angel Of Harlem' (follow-up to 'Desire', both in 1988), 'When Love Comes To Town' (with BB King - April 1989), 'All I Want Is You' (June 1989)

DURAN DURAN

1. What was the title of the group's first Top 20 hit?

2. On which Caribbean island did Duran Duran film the video for their single 'Rio'?

3. The group had two number one singles in the UK. The second was 'The Reflex'. What was the title of the first?

4. In America, they also achieved two number one hits with 'The Reflex' and which other song?

5. Can you name the act featured on Duran Duran's 1995 Top 20 cover of 'White Lines (Don't Do It)'?

6. Simon Le Bon, Nick Rhodes and Roger Taylor made the Top 10 in 1985 as Arcadia, but what was the title of the song?

7 Andy Taylor and John Taylor were part of a group that had a Top 20 hit in 1985 with 'Some Like It Hot'. Can you name that group?

8 In 2004, the group made the Top 5 with their single 'Sunrise', but what four words in brackets preceded the main title?

9 Who co-produced the 1986 album *Notorious* with the band?

10 Making the Top 40 in 1989, what is the title of their song that featured in the Mel Gibson movie *Tequila Sunrise*?

ANSWERS TO 1989

1. 'If You Don't Know Me By Now' 2. Prince 3. 'Losing My Mind' (produced by Pet Shop Boys & Julian Mendelsohn) 4. Caron Wheeler 5. 'What I Am' (Tin Tin Out featuring Emma Bunton) 6. Chris Rea 7. Thompson Twins (written by Alannah Currie and Tom Bailey) 8. 'That's What I Like', 'Let's Party' 9. 'Days' 10. S'Express

EURYTHMICS

1. What was the title of Eurythmics' only American number one?

2. The song 'Put A Little Love In Your Heart' was a 1988 Top 40 duet by Annie Lennox and which other singer?

3. Although different songs, what three-word title gave Eurythmics a Top 3 hit in 1983 and Madonna a number one in 1987?

4. Though signed to RCA Records, their single 'Sexcrime (Nineteen Eighty-Four)' was released on which other label?

5. While members of The Tourists, which sixties hit for Dusty Springfield did they take back into the Top 5 in 1979?

6 Under what pseudonym did Dave Stewart co-write Shakespears Sister's 1992 number one, 'Stay'?

7 Eurythmics only had one Top 20 hit in the nineties, can you name that song?

8 What instrument did Annie Lennox play when she was in the seventies group Dragon's Playground?

9 Dave Stewart and Terry Hall recorded their 1992 hit 'Possessed' under what name?

10 What is the title of the only UK number one hit single achieved by the duo?

ANSWERS TO DURAN DURAN

1. 'Planet Earth' 2. Antigua 3. 'Is There Something I Should Know' 4. 'A View To A Kill' 5. Melle Mel & Grandmaster Flash and The Furious Five 6. 'Election Day' 7. The Power Station 8. '(Reach Up For The) Sunrise' 9. Nile Rodgers 10. 'Do You Believe In Shame'

PET SHOP BOYS

1. Which 1986 Top 20 single has the subtitle '(Let's Make Lots Of Money)'?

2. As a teenager, Chris Lowe played in a dance band called One Under The Eight. Which instrument did he play?

3. Neil and Chris wrote (and co-produced with Phil Harding) 'I'm Not Scared', a hit for Eighth Wonder. Who was the group's lead singer?

4. In 2004, Pet Shop Boys composed music to accompany a 1925 silent film by the Russian director Sergei Eisenstein. It was released as an album the following year. What was the film called?

5. Prior to his success with Chris Lowe, Neil had been an editor at which pop magazine?

6 All of the duo's studio albums have one-word titles. Which was the first, released in 1986?

7 Their song 'Confidential' appeared on the 1996 album *Wildest Dreams*, recorded by which singer?

8 Pet Shop Boys both featured on and co-wrote the 2007 hit 'She's Madonna' by which singer?

9 What is the name of the record label they formed in the early nineties, that had a Top 20 hit with the song 'Love Is Everywhere' by Cicero?

10 The song 'Love Comes Quickly' includes the saxophone played by a member of Roxy Music. Who is he?

ANSWERS TO EURYTHMICS

1. 'Sweet Dreams (Are Made Of This)' 2. Al Green 3. 'Who's That Girl?' (Madonna's number one doesn't have the question mark!) 4. Virgin 5. 'I Only Want To Be With You' 6. Jean Guiot 7. 'I Saved The World Today' 8. Flute 9. Vegas 10. 'There Must Be An Angel (Playing With My Heart)'

PRINCE

1. In 1985, 'Let's Go Crazy' reached the Top 10 alongside which other song from the *Purple Rain* album?

2. What was unusual about the original CD release of his 1988 album *Lovesexy*?

3. The first single from his 1996 triple album *Emancipation*, released during the period when he abandoned the name Prince, was a Top 20 cover of a song made famous by The Stylistics. What is the song?

4. Sheena Easton is featured on the 1987 single 'U Got The Look', but she also duetted with Prince on a 1989 single taken from his *Batman* album. What is the song?

5. In which American state was he born, that was also home to his Paisley Park Studios?

6 In 1993, Prince played keyboards, guitar, bass and provided vocals on 'Why Should I Love You?', a song that featured on the album *The Red Shoes* by which artist?

7 Tom Jones had a Top 5 hit in 1988 with Prince's song 'Kiss', where he was billed alongside which other chart act?

8 Which 1991 album included the singles 'Cream', 'Gett Off' and 'Money Don't Matter 2 Night'?

9 Prince reached the Top 40 for the first time in 1983 with which single?

10 What was his surname and in which year was he born?

ANSWERS TO PET SHOP BOYS

1. 'Opportunities (Let's Make Lots Of Money)' 2. Trombone 3. Patsy Kensit 4. *Battleship Potemkin* 5. *Smash Hits* 6. *Please* 7. Tina Turner 8. Robbie Williams 9. Spaghetti 10. Andy Mackay

WHITNEY HOUSTON

1. Which number one by Whitney has the words '(Who Loves Me)' at the end of its title?

2. Whitney's final Top 40 hit of the eighties was titled 'It Isn't, It Wasn't, It Ain't Never Gonna Be' and was a duet with which legendary soul singer?

3. The mid-nineties hit 'Exhale (Shoop Shoop)' and her duet with CeCe Winans called 'Count On Me' were featured on the soundtrack to which movie starring Whitney and Angela Bassett?

4. Co-written by Whitney and co-produced by Bobby Brown, which 2002 Top 20 hit was her response to what she felt was media criticism of her?

5. Whitney reached the Top 10 in 1986 with 'Greatest Love Of All', a cover of a 1977 hit for which singer and guitarist?

6. Which successful singer and pianist was a co-writer on Whitney's 2009 Top 5 song 'Million Dollar Bill'?

7 Although different songs, which 1993 Top 20 single by Whitney has the same three-word title as the 1985 Top 20 hit by Bryan Adams?

8 The producer of her 1986 Top 10 single 'How Will I Know' had reached the Top 10 himself in 1980 with the song 'I Shoulda Loved Ya'. Who is he?

9 Which of her hits was used by America's NBC TV network for their coverage of the 1988 Olympic Games?

10 One of Whitney's earliest recordings was singing lead vocals on 'Life's A Party', the 1978 single and album title track by which producer and performer?

ANSWERS TO PRINCE

1. 'Take Me With U' (Some pressings listed as double A-side, some 'A' and 'B', some 'Side 1' and 'Side 2'. But both songs are officially listed.) 2. The whole album (nine songs) was (deliberately) pressed as a single track. 3. 'Betcha By Golly Wow!' 4. 'The Arms Of Orion' 5. Minnesota 6. Kate Bush 7. The Art of Noise 8. *Diamonds And Pearls* 9. '1999' 10. Nelson, 1958

1990s GOLDEN YEARS

Baggy jeans, bucket hats, tie-dye, scrunchies and butterfly clips, *Art Attack*, *Live & Kicking*, *Fantomcat*, *Get Your Own Back* and *Demon Headmaster*.

1990s POPMASTER 1

1. What was the title of the 1998 number one by Run-DMC vs Jason Nevins?
2. The songs 'Don't Be A Stranger' and 'The Perfect Year' were hits in 1993 for which British singer?
3. What '_____ Thing' did Jesus Jones sing about, according to the title of the group's 1991 Top 10 single?
4. Which group's hits in the early nineties included 'No Son Of Mine' and 'Hold On My Heart'?
5. Roxette had a Top 10 hit in both 1990 and 1993 with the song 'It Must Have _____' what?
6. Who wanted to 'Save The Best For Last' according to the title of her 1992 Top 3 song?

7 'What Is Love', Haddaway's Top 3 chart debut in 1993, was the first of four Top 10 singles for the singer in the nineties. Can you name one of the other three?

8 The songs 'She's A River' and 'Hypnotised' reached the charts in 1995 for which Scottish band?

9 What is the one-word title of both the 1991 Top 10 single by Sabrina Johnston and the final studio album by Eurythmics, which was Top 5 in 1999?

10 The single 'Jump Around' reached the Top 40 in 1992, but then became a Top 10 single in 1993 when it was re-issued alongside the song 'Top Of The Morning To Ya'. Which hip-hop act recorded it?

ANSWERS TO WHITNEY HOUSTON

1. 'I Wanna Dance With Somebody (Who Loves Me)' 2. Aretha Franklin (taken from Franklin's album *Through The Storm*) 3. *Waiting To Exhale* 4. 'Whatchulookinat' 5. George Benson (Benson's title officially 'The Greatest Love Of All') 6. Alicia Keys 7. 'Run To You' 8. Narada Michael Walden 9. 'One Moment In Time' 10. Michael Zager (The Michael Zager Band)

1990s POPMASTER 2

1 'Auberge' was the title of both a hit single and number one album in 1991 for which singer and guitarist?

2 Which Tracy Chapman song was covered by Boyzone for a Top 3 single in 1997?

3 Featuring vocals by Duane Harden, which American DJ and producer reached number one in 1999 with his track 'You Don't Know Me'?

4 American singer Jennifer Paige made her only UK Top 40 appearance in 1998, with a Top 5 song that had a one-word title. What is that title?

5 The Chemical Brothers had two number one singles in the nineties. 'Block Rockin' Beats' was the second of these. What was the first?

6 Who had a Top 5 single with 'Peacock Suit' in 1996?

7 Which Small Faces song was covered by M People in 1995?

8 Whose Top 10 singles during the 1990s included 'Thought I'd Died And Gone To Heaven', 'Cloud Number 9' and 'The Only Thing That Looks Good On Me Is You'?

9 The singer Shanice reached number two in 1992 with which song?

10 Who had a Top 20 single in 1993 called 'Now I Know What Made Otis Blue'?

ANSWERS TO 1990s POPMASTER 1

1. 'It's Like That' 2. Dina Carroll 3. 'International Bright Young Thing' 4. Genesis 5. 'It Must Have Been Love' 6. Vanessa Williams 7. 'Life' (No. 6 in 1993), 'I Miss You' (released 1993, peaked at No. 9 early 1994), 'Rock My Heart' (No. 9 in 1994) 8. Simple Minds 9. 'Peace' 10. House Of Pain

1990s POPMASTER 3

1. A song about a dance craze gave Los Del Rio a massive international hit in 1996. What was it called?

2. The songs 'When' and 'From This Moment On' were hits in 1998 for which singer?

3. Despite a run of Top 10 singles in the late eighties, Rick Astley had just one Top 10 single in the nineties. What was it called?

4. In 1995, which group had a Top 10 album called *Beggar On A Beach Of Gold* and a Top 40 single called 'A Beggar On A Beach Of Gold'?

5. Originally released in 1993, what is the one-word title of the 1994 Top 40 debut by The Cranberries?

6. Which band's hits in the nineties included 'Anybody Seen My Baby?', 'I Go Wild' and 'Saint Of Me'?

7 In 1991, Pet Shop Boys reached the Top 5 with a medley that consisted of 'Where The Streets Have No Name' and which other song?

8 The singles 'At The River' and 'If Everybody Looked The Same' were hits for the chart act formed by Andy Cato and Tom Findlay. What is the name of the act?

9 The songs 'I Am, I Feel' and 'The Incidentals' were two of the hits in the second half of the nineties by which duo?

10 In 1999, Andy Williams reached the Top 10 for the first time in two and a half decades with which song?

ANSWERS TO 1990s POPMASTER 2

1. Chris Rea 2. 'Baby Can I Hold You' 3. Armand Van Helden 4. 'Crush' 5. 'Setting Sun' 6. Paul Weller 7. 'Itchycoo Park' 8. Bryan Adams 9. 'I Love Your Smile' 10. Paul Young

1990s POPMASTER 4

1. Who had an 'Achy Breaky Heart', according to the title of his 1992 Top 3 song?

2. The singer Ultra Naté had two Top 10 singles in the nineties. Can you name either of them?

3. In 1999, Tony Christie reached the Top 10 as vocalist on 'Walk Like A Panther', a song recorded by which chart act?

4. The title of which 1991 Top 20 single by MC Hammer ends with the word 'Hammer'?

5. Which short-lived boy band had all four of their Top 40 hits in 1996, beginning with the Top 20 song 'Change Your Mind' and ending with a Top 30 cover of Chicago's 'If You Leave Me Now'?

6. Having reached the Top 10 in 1989 with 'Right Here Waiting', Richard Marx had his only other Top 10 single in 1992. What is it called?

7 A song written and recorded by David McWilliams in the sixties became a Top 5 hit for Marc Almond in the early nineties. What is it called?

8 'Erase/Rewind' is the title of a 1999 Top 10 single by which Scandinavian group?

9 The songs 'Light Of My Life', 'Arms Around The World' and 'Undivided Love' were all Top 10 solo singles in the nineties for which singer?

10 Which country provides the title of the 1997 Top 3 single by Sash! featuring Rodriguez?

ANSWERS TO 1990s POPMASTER 3

1. 'Macarena' 2. Shania Twain 3. 'Cry For Help' 4. Mike + The Mechanics 5. 'Linger' 6. Rolling Stones 7. 'Can't Take My Eyes Off You' (The medley was a double A-side with 'How Can You Expect To Be Taken Seriously?'.) 8. Groove Armada 9. Alisha's Attic 10. 'Music To Watch Girls By' (His previous Top 10 hit was 'Solitaire', released in 1973 and Top 10 in January 1974.)

1990s POPMASTER 5

1. Who reached number one in 1999 with 'Livin' La Vida Loca'?

2. Tori Amos had a Top 10 single in 1994 called 'Pretty Good _____' what?

3. 'Unskinny Bop' was a hit in 1990 for which American band?

4. Beverley Craven first reached the Top 40 in 1991 with her Top 3 song 'Promise Me'. She went on to have three further Top 40 hits during the decade. Can you name one of them?

5. The songs 'Barrel Of A Gun' and 'It's No Good' were both Top 5 in 1997 for which group?

6. 'Blue Room', 'Little Fluffy Clouds' and 'Toxygene' were all Top 10 singles in the nineties for which chart act?

7 Cliff Richard's first Top 10 of the nineties was a live version of a song that had been Top 3 for Herman's Hermits in 1965. What is the song?

8 What 'Book _____' did Enya sing about on her 1992 single?

9 'Better Off Alone' and 'Back In My Life' were both Top 5 in 1999 for a Eurodance/pop project formed by a group of musicians, DJs and producers in the Netherlands. Under what name do they record?

10 Who had hits in 1996 called 'If It Makes You Happy' and 'Everyday Is A Winding Road'?

ANSWERS TO 1990s POPMASTER 4

1. Billy Ray Cyrus 2. 'Free' (No. 4 in 1997), 'Found A Cure' (No. 6 in 1998) 3. The All Seeing I 4. 'Here Comes The Hammer' (That same year he had a Top 20 single called '(Hammer Hammer) They Put Me In The Mix'.) 5. Upside Down 6. 'Hazard' 7. 'The Days Of Pearly Spencer' 8. The Cardigans 9. Louise 10. 'Ecuador'

1990s POPMASTER 6

1. A remixed version of which seventies hit by Free returned to the Top 10 in 1991?

2. 'Breakfast At Tiffany's' was a 1996 number one for which American rock band?

3. The group Lovestation had both of its Top 20 hits in 1998. Can you name either of them?

4. What is the name of the saxophonist who featured on Michael Bolton's 1992 single 'Missing You Now'?

5. American group De'Lacy made their chart debut in 1995 with which Top 10 hit?

6. In 1996, which singer reached the Top 40 with her version of Gene Pitney's hit 'Town Without Pity'?

7. Which rap artist featured on Blackstreet's 1996 Top 10 single 'No Diggity'?

8. Which 1997 Top 3 single by Boyzone featured on the soundtrack to *Bean: The Ultimate Disaster Movie*?

9. What was the title of the only major hit by Opus III, which reached the Top 5 in 1992?

10. The singles 'I Want You Back' and 'Tearin' Up My Heart' were both first released in 1997, but both failed to make the Top 10 until they were re-issued in 1999. Which boy band recorded these hits?

ANSWERS TO 1990s POPMASTER 5

1. Ricky Martin 2. 'Pretty Good Year' 3. Poison 4. 'Holding On', 'Woman To Woman' (both 1991), 'Love Scenes' (1993) 5. Depeche Mode 6. The Orb 7. 'Silhouettes' 8. 'Book Of Days' 9. Alice Deejay 10. Sheryl Crow

1990s POPMASTER 7

1. What 1998 number one by Oasis has the same title as a 1989 number one by Lisa Stansfield?

2. With which successful American rap and hip hop act do you associate Wyclef Jean, Pras Michel and Lauryn Hill?

3. In 1997, Orbital had two consecutive Top 10 hits. The first was a live version of the duo's 1991 hit 'Satan'. What was the other?

4. Can you name the female singer-songwriter who had a Top 10 album in 1990 called *Days Of Open Hand*?

5. A dance version of 'I Will Always Love You' was a Top 20 single in 1993 for Sarah _____ who?

6 Which one of these three hits by U2 gained the highest chart position: 'Who's Gonna Ride Your Wild Horses', 'Mysterious Ways' or 'Sweetest Thing'?

7 Can you name the performer who entered the Top 40 at number one in 1998 with 'You Make Me Wanna...'?

8 Ozzy Osbourne and Kim Basinger were uncredited vocalists on a 1992 Top 5 single by Was (Not Was). What was it called?

9 A cover of which classic Bob Dylan song was a hit for The Rolling Stones in 1995?

10 Reaching the Top 20 in 1997, 'Night Nurse' by Sly and Robbie also featured which successful chart act?

ANSWERS TO 1990s POPMASTER 6

1. 'All Right Now' 2. Deep Blue Something 3. 'Teardrops', 'Sensuality' 4. Kenny G 5. 'Hideaway' 6. Eddi Reader 7. Dr Dre 8. 'Picture Of You' 9. 'It's A Fine Day' 10. 'N Sync

1990s POPMASTER 8

1. Which boy band entered the charts at number one in 1999 with 'Keep On Moving'?

2. Who featured alongside Maxi Priest on the 1996 Top 20 single 'That Girl'?

3. Which 1991 Top 10 single by De La Soul has the bracketed subtitle '(Ha Ha Hey)'?

4. What was the title of Neneh Cherry's only solo Top 10 song during the nineties?

5. Kim Appleby achieved two Top 10 hits in 1990 and 1991 respectively. The first was 'Don't Worry'. What was the title of the second?

6. Can you name the Northern Irish act whose single 'The Pop Singer's Fear Of The Pollen Count' reached the Top 20 in 1999?

7 Which one of these three hits by Cher gained the highest chart position? Was it 'Strong Enough', 'Just Like Jesse James' or 'Love And Understanding'?

8 Rod Stewart's 1978 single 'Da Ya Think I'm Sexy' was a hit all over again in 1997, when samples of his number one featured on a Top 10 version of the song by which UK group?

9 Finishing in tenth place, Samantha Janus represented the UK in the 1991 Eurovision Song Contest with which Top 40 song?

10 Which band had a number one album in 1996 simply called *K*?

ANSWERS TO 1990s POPMASTER 7

1. 'All Around The World' 2. Fugees 3. 'The Saint' 4. Suzanne Vega 5. Sarah Washington 6. 'Sweetest Thing' (Reached No. 3, 'Who's Gonna Ride Your Wild Horses' No. 14, 'Mysterious Ways' No. 13.) 7. Usher (The European version of the single had charted outside the Top 75 as an import prior to its official UK release.) 8. 'Shake Your Head' 9. 'Like A Rolling Stone' 10. Simply Red

1990s POPMASTER 9

1. Which group topped the charts in 1990 with 'A Little Time'?

2. In 1991, PM Dawn had a Top 3 single called 'Set Adrift On Memory Bliss'. It featured a sample from a 1983 number one. What was that number one?

3. Can you name the actor who made the Top 5 in 1998 with a cover of Leo Sayer's 1977 number one, 'When I Need You'?

4. In 1995, Supergrass had a Top 3 hit with their double A-side 'Alright' and which other one-word song?

5. Finishing in second place, Michael Ball represented the UK in the 1992 Eurovision Song Contest with which Top 20 song?

6. Featuring singer Melanie Williams, which chart act had a Top 3 single in 1993 called 'Ain't No Love (Ain't No Use)'?

7 Cappella had three Top 10 hits in the nineties that began with the letter 'U'. The first was 'U Got 2 Know', but can you name either of the other two?

8 'Who Am I (Sim Simma)' was a 1998 Top 10 single for which Jamaican singer, rapper and dancehall DJ?

9 Can you name the group that had a 1991 Top 3 album called *Fellow Hoodlums*?

10 'Spaceman' was a 1996 number one for Babylon Zoo. The chart act made its only two other Top 40 appearances that same year. Can you name one of them?

ANSWERS TO 1990s POPMASTER 8

1. Five 2. Shaggy 3. 'Ring Ring Ring (Ha Ha Hey)' 4. 'Woman' (She also reached the Top 10 with Youssou N'Dour with '7 Seconds' and No. 1 with Cher, Chrissie Hynde and Eric Clapton with 'Love Can Build A Bridge'.) 5. 'G.L.A.D' 6. The Divine Comedy 7. 'Strong Enough' (Reached No. 5, 'Just Like Jesse James' No. 11, 'Love And Understanding' No. 10.) 8. N-Trance 9. 'A Message To Your Heart' 10. Kula Shaker

1990s POPMASTER 10

1. Released in 1999, *The Slim Shady LP* was a hit album for which American rapper?

2. The first three chart hits for Aqua all reached number one in the late nineties. 'Barbie Girl' was the first, but can you name either of the other two?

3. With which group did Vic Reeves reach number one in 1991 with a version of Tommy Roe's 1969 number one 'Dizzy'?

4. What was the title of the 1997 Top 20 chart debut by Steps?

5. The songs 'Human Touch', 'The Ghost of Tom Joad' and 'Secret Garden' were all hits in the nineties for which star?

6 Although different songs, what hit title was shared by a 1996 Top 5 single for Livin' Joy and a number one in 2001 by S Club 7?

7 Which brotherly trio entered the album charts at number one in 1997 with *Middle Of Nowhere*?

8 Actor Jimmy Nail had a number one single in 1992 with which song?

9 By what name are the duo Ed Simons and Tom Rowlands better known?

10 Only one solo single released by Robbie Williams in the nineties failed to make the Top 10. What is it called?

ANSWERS TO 1990s POPMASTER 9

1. The Beautiful South 2. 'True' by Spandau Ballet 3. Will Mellor 4. 'Time' 5. 'One Step Out Of Time' 6. Sub Sub 7. 'U Got 2 Let The Music', 'U & Me' 8. Beenie Man 9. Deacon Blue 10. 'Animal Army', 'The Boy With The X-Ray Eyes'

1990

1. Cliff Richard had the Christmas number one this year with which song?

2. Which footballer performed the rap on Englandneworder's 'World In Motion'?

3. A recording of a live concert by The Three Tenors spent a total of five weeks as the UK's number one album. Luciano Pavarotti and Placido Domingo were two of the three tenors. Who was the third?

4. What was the title of Prince's 1990 film and soundtrack album, seen as a sequel to *Purple Rain*?

5. Maria McKee reached number one with 'Show Me Heaven', but prior to her solo career she had been a founding member of which 'Cowpunk' band?

6. Following her lead vocal on Beats International's number one 'Dub Be Good To Me', Lindy Layton had another Top 40 hit this year, with a cover of a 1979 Top 3 single. Lindy's version featured the singer of that original hit. What is the song and who was the original singer?

7 Abel Makkonen Tesfaye was born in February 1990 and went on to become one of Canada's most successful acts of the 2010s. Who is he?

8 David Lynch's TV series *Twin Peaks* aired this year. A vocal version of its theme tune was a Top 10 hit. What is the title of this vocal version and who sang it?

9 DJ & producer Chad Jackson had his only Top 40 hit with a Top 3 track subtitled '(Get Wicked)'. What is its full title?

10 1990 was the most successful chart year for Betty Boo as an artist. But under her real name, she's co-written songs for Girls Aloud, Hear'Say, Louise and Paloma Faith amongst others. What is her real name?

ANSWERS TO 1990s POPMASTER 10

1. Eminem 2. 'Doctor Jones' and 'Turn Back Time' 3. The Wonder Stuff 4. '5,6,7,8' 5. Bruce Springsteen 6. 'Don't Stop Movin' 7. Hanson 8. 'Ain't No Doubt' 9. The Chemical Brothers 10. 'South Of The Border' (reached No. 14 in 1997)

1991

1. Massive Attack released the seminal track 'Unfinished Sympathy' under the name Massive. Who sang lead vocal and went on to solo success this decade?

2. Madonna's film *In Bed With Madonna* premiered this year. It came out under a different title in America. What is that alternative title?

3. The Prodigy had its debut hit in 1991 with a Top 3 single that sampled a public information film from the seventies. What is the title of this debut hit?

4. Sally Herbert and Caroline Buckley had been musicians in The Communards before forming a duo in the early nineties and having a hit this year with 'This Is Your Life'. Under what name did they record this single?

5. 'Do The Bartman' was number one for The Simpsons. But there was a Top 10 follow-up the same year. What was it called?

6 Can you name the Italian group that reached the Top 3 with a dance version of the Christopher Cross song 'Ride Like The Wind'?

7 Dire Straits released their final studio album in 1991. It included the Top 40 single 'Calling Elvis'. What is the album called?

8 'Always Look On The Bright Side Of Life' was Top 10 for Monty Python this year. But which member of the Python team both wrote and sang the song?

9 The Top 10 song 'Hippychick' by Soho sampled Johnny Marr's guitar from which Smiths song?

10 'Radio Wall Of Sound' was Slade's final original chart hit. Which member of the band is the main vocalist on the song?

ANSWERS TO 1990

1. 'Saviour's Day' 2. John Barnes 3. José Carreras 4. *Graffiti Bridge* 5. Lone Justice 6. 'Silly Games' - Janet Kay 7. The Weekend 8. 'Falling' - Julee Cruise 9. 'Hear The Drummer (Get Wicked)' 10. Alison Clarkson

1992

1 Annie Lennox released her debut solo album this year. It sold over a million copies in the UK. What was it called?

2 Which American band made their chart debut this year with the Top 3 song 'To Be With You'?

3 The Freddie Mercury Tribute Concert for Aids Awareness took place on 20 April. Paul Young, Seal and Lisa Stansfield were three of the guest vocalists with Queen, but which songs did they sing solo with the band?

4 Pettigrew and Chacon are the surnames of the duo that reached number one with 'Would I Lie To You?'. It was released under their first names. What was the duo called?

5 Steve Mac, who has co-written the number ones 'Shape of You' by Ed Sheeran, 'Symphony' by Clean Bandit with Zara Larsson and 'The Club Is Alive' by JLS amongst others, was in the Top 10 this year as one third of a group that recorded a dance version of Andrew Gold's 'Never Let Her Slip Away'. What were they called?

6 The film *Batman Returns* was released this year. Its soundtrack was written by Danny Elfman,

but it also includes a hit song by Siouxsie and the Banshees, which they co-wrote with the composer. What is it called?

7 Which group had the only Top 40 hit of its chart career this year with the song 'Highway 5'?

8 Erasure spent five weeks at number one with their *ABBA-esque* EP. Of the four ABBA songs on the release, only one had been a UK number one for the Swedish group. What is that song?

9 The American group that had a Top 3 single called 'People Everyday' have the same name as an American sitcom from the noughties starring Jason Bateman and Portia de Rossi. What is that shared name?

10 The Mercury Music Prize (now known as the Mercury Prize) was awarded for the first time this year. Who won it and what was the title of the album?

ANSWERS TO 1991

1. Shara Nelson 2. *Madonna: Truth or Dare* 3. 'Charly' 4. Banderas 5. 'Deep Deep Trouble' 6. East Side Beat 7. *On Every Street* 8. Eric Idle 9. 'How Soon Is Now?' ('Hippychick' had originally been released in the spring of 1990 but failed to reach the Top 40. It only became a Top 10 hit on its 1991 re-entry.) 10. Jim Lea (Noddy Holder joined in on the choruses.)

1993

1. Who had the UK's biggest selling single and album of the year, and what is the title of both of these?

2. 'Cherub Rock' is the title of the first Top 40 single by which American band?

3. Björk's Top 40 solo career began this year with 'Human Behaviour'. But she had reached the Top 40 the previous year as a member of an Icelandic band. What is the name of that band and what is the one-word title of their only Top 40 hit?

4. The Bluebells spent a month at number one with the song 'Young At Heart'. But the single had already been Top 10 for the group some years earlier. In which year was it originally a hit and, for an extra point, which member of Bananarama is credited as co-writer on its 1993 release?

5. Under what name did Canadian rapper Darrin O'Brien record his Top 3 hit and American number one, 'Informer'?

6. The Bee Gees had two Top 40 hits this year, both of which had five-word titles. Can you

name either of them? (An extra point if you can name both!).

7 The vocal group SWV reached the charts for the first time with the Top 20 song 'I'm So Into You', but what does SWV stand for?

8 Boy band East 17 released their number one debut album this year. What was it called?

9 The songs 'Alone' and 'Ships (Where Were You)' were the final two Top 40 hits for a band that had debuted on the chart ten years earlier. What was the band called?

10 The song that had the most UK radio airplay in 1993 was Billy Joel's only Top 10 single of the decade. What was the song called?

ANSWERS TO 1992

1. *Diva* 2. Mr. Big 3. Paul Young sang 'Radio Ga Ga', Seal sang 'Who Wants To Live Forever', Lisa Stansfield sang 'I Want To Break Free'. (Lisa also joined George Michael and Queen for 'These Are The Days Of Our Lives'.) 4. Charles & Eddie 5. Undercover 6. 'Face To Face' 7. The Blessing ('Highway 5' was originally released in 1991 but didn't reach the Top 40. It was remixed and became a Top 40 hit in 1992.) 8. 'Take A Chance On Me'. The other three songs on the EP were 'Lay All Your Love On Me' (No. 7), 'SOS' (No. 6) and 'Voulez-Vous' (No. 3). 9. Arrested Development 10. Primal Scream for *Screamadelica*

1994

1. Elton John wrote songs for *The Lion King* with which lyricist?

2. Released this year, what is the title of the film based on The Beatles' early years in Hamburg, starring Stephen Dorff, Sheryl Lee and Ian Hart?

3. Which American gospel group is featured alongside Daryl Hall on the Top 40 hit 'Gloryland'?

4. Beginning with the earliest, put these four songs in the order they were number one this year: 'Let Me Be Your Fantasy' by Baby D, 'The Real Thing' by Tony Di Bart, 'Without You' by Mariah Carey and 'Saturday Night' by Whigfield?

5. Having played Aidan Brosnan on *EastEnders* throughout 1993, which actor had the first of eight Top 40 hits in the summer of 1994 with 'Someone To Love'?

6. A Scottish band reached number one in May 1994 with a song that featured in a TV commercial for a popular brand of denim jeans. What is the name of both the band and the number one single?

7 The Beautiful South released their first ever 'Best Of' album in November. It became the bestselling album by a British act in 1994. Its title was quintessentially British. What was it called?

8 As the K Foundation, which chart act reportedly burnt a million pounds they'd earned in royalties?

9 Cyndi Lauper had a Top 5 single with a new recording of her 1984 hit 'Girls Just Want To Have Fun'. The song's original title was used as a subtitle for this 10th anniversary version. What is the full title of this 1994 recording?

10 Ireland became the first country to win the Eurovision Song Contest in three consecutive years with 'Why Me?' by Linda Martin in 1992, 'In Your Eyes' by Niamh Kavanagh in 1993, and which song and act in 1994?

ANSWERS TO 1993

1. Meat Loaf with 'I'd Do Anything For Love (But I Won't Do That)' from the album *Bat Out Of Hell II – Back To Hell*. 2. Smashing Pumpkins 3. The Sugarcubes – 'Hit' 4. 1984 – Siobhan Fahey (of Bananarama & Shakespears Sister) 5. Snow 6. 'Paying The Price Of Love', 'For Whom The Bell Tolls' 7. Sisters With Voices 8. *Walthamstow* (the town in Greater London with the postcode E17) 9. Big Country 10. 'The River Of Dreams'

1995

1. Who wrote Tina Turner's theme song to the James Bond film *Goldeneye*?

2. Pulp's single 'Sorted For E's and Whizz' was a double A-side with which other song?

3. What are the surnames of Robson and Jerome who had number ones this year with 'Unchained Melody'/'(There'll Be Bluebirds Over) The White Cliffs Of Dover' and 'I Believe'/'Up On The Roof'?

4. In 1995, four years after his death, Queen released the final studio album to feature Freddie Mercury's vocals. What was it called?

5. Beginning with the earliest, put these four songs in the order they were number one this year: 'Cotton Eye Joe' by Rednex, 'Dreamer' by Livin' Joy, 'Gangsta's Paradise' by Coolio featuring LV and 'Never Forget' by Take That.

6. Which R&B/pop group had Top 10 hits this year with 'I've Got A Little Something For You', 'If You Only Let Me In' and 'Happy'?

7 Written by Ellie Greenwich, the singer Berri had a Top 5 dance version of an Elkie Brooks hit from the seventies. What is the song?

8 Sonia Madan is lead singer with the band that had Top 30 singles in 1995 with 'Great Things' and 'King Of The Kerb'. What is the name of the band?

9 A demo recording in the seventies by John Lennon was completed by the three remaining Beatles and released as a single in December this year. It entered the charts at number two. What was it called, and for a bonus point, which song and artist stopped it entering the chart at number one?

10 What 1995 single by Cher was a cover of a Top 30 song for its writer Marc Cohn in 1991?

ANSWERS TO 1994

1. Tim Rice 2. *Backbeat* 3. Sounds of Blackness 4. 'Without You' (February), 'The Real Thing' (May), 'Saturday Night (September), 'Let Me Be Your Fantasy' (November) 5. Sean Maguire 6. Stiltskin with 'Inside' 7. *Carry On Up The Charts* (This was the second bestselling album of the year. No. 1 was *Cross Road: The Best Of Bon Jovi*.) 8. The KLF 9. 'Hey Now (Girls Just Want To Have Fun)' 10. 'Rock N' Roll Kids' by Paul Harrington and Charlie McGettigan

1996

1. Which seventies band reformed for the Filthy Lucre Tour this year?

2. The critically acclaimed film *Trainspotting* was released this year. What Iggy Pop song is featured in the film's opening sequence and which Underworld track features in its closing scene?

3. What was Victoria Beckham's surname at the time of the Spice Girls' debut number one 'Wannabe'?

4. George Michael's number one 'Fastlove' includes a reference to a 1982 Top 10 song by an American singer. What is that Top 10 song and who sang it?

5. 'I've Got A Little Puppy' and 'Your Christmas Wish' were both Top 10 singles this year for which chart act?

6. American composer Mark Snow had a Top 3 single with his theme music to one of the most popular TV series of the mid-nineties. What is it called?

7 Which Chicago-born R&B singer had a hit ballad version of Gloria Gaynor's number one 'I Will Survive'?

8 The band Ocean Colour Scene released their multi-platinum album *Moseley Shoals* this year including four hit singles. 'The Riverboat Song' was Top 20. The other three all reached the Top 10. Can you name one of these?

9 Michael Jackson's nephews (sons of Tito Jackson) had their most successful chart year with a Top 20 single and three Top 3 hits. They were called 3T due to their names being Taj (Tariano), T.J. (Tito) and _____ what?

10 The duo Spiro and Wix reached the charts with music used for the BBC's coverage of the Olympic Games in Atlanta. Called 'Tara's Theme', it was a reworking of music composed by Max Steiner for which classic film?

ANSWERS TO 1995

1. Bono and The Edge 2. 'Mis-Shapes' 3. Robson Green & Jerome Flynn (debut hit released as Robson Green & Jerome Flynn, subsequent releases just Robson & Jerome) 4. *Made in Heaven* 5. 'Cotton Eye Joe' (January), 'Dreamer' (May), 'Never Forget' (August), 'Gangsta's Paradise' (October) 6. MN8 7. 'Sunshine After The Rain' (Berri's dance version was called 'The Sunshine After The Rain'.) 8. Echobelly 9. 'Free As A Bird' (kept from No. 1 by 'Earth Song' by Michael Jackson) 10. 'Walking In Memphis'

1997

1 The third album by Oasis was released this year and broke records as the fastest selling album in UK chart history. What was it called?

2 Which singer made her Top 40 debut in 1997 with a Top 5 version of the Randy Crawford hit 'You Might Need Somebody'?

3 The soundtrack to the film *The Full Monty* included Tom Jones covering a song written and recorded by Randy Newman on his 1972 album *Sail Away*. It was released as a single but didn't chart, although it has remained popular with his audience. What is the song?

4 The Top 3 song 'Freed From Desire' has become a favourite celebration song at sporting events in recent years. It was recorded by which Italian singer?

5 Which hit single by Aerosmith has the subtitle '(Is Hard On The Knees)'?

6 Channel 5 TV launched this year and in its first week aired a brand-new music show called *Night Fever*. Based around karaoke, it

was presented by a well-known singer from a popular band. Who is he?

7 The singer-songwriter Conner Reeves made his chart debut with a Top 20 song called 'My Father's _____' what?

8 Spike, Lee and Jimmy had Top 5 singles this year called 'The Day We Find Love', 'Bodyshakin', 'The Journey' and 'Party People...Friday Night'. Under what name did they record these songs?

9 Composer David Arnold along with Propellerheads had a Top 10 hit with their version of which James Bond theme?

10 Placebo, The Foo Fighters, Lou Reed and Robert Smith of the Cure were among the artists appearing at Madison Square Garden in New York at the fiftieth birthday concert of which superstar?

ANSWERS TO 1996

1. The Sex Pistols 2. 'Lust For Life' (Iggy Pop), 'Born Slippy' (Underworld) 3. Victoria Adams 4. 'Forget Me Nots' by Patrice Rushen 5. The Smurfs 6. *The X Files* 7. Chantay Savage 8. 'You've Got It Bad' (No. 7), 'The Day We Caught The Train' (No. 4), 'The Circle' (No. 6) 9. Taryll 10. *Gone with the Wind*

1998

1. Although it only reached number four, which Robbie Williams single was the number one airplay hit of the year?

2. Which politician got a soaking from Chumbawamba at the Brit Awards this year?

3. Boyzone's 1998 number one 'No Matter What' is a song that originally featured in a musical by Andrew Lloyd Webber and Jim Steinman. What is the name of the musical?

4. At 15, who became the youngest British solo artist to have a debut hit enter the chart at number one and what was the title of her song?

5. The song 'Islands In The Stream' was interpolated on a Top 3 single by a member of Fugees (and featuring ODB & Mya). Who is that Fugees member and what is the title of the single?

6. Sisters Cleo, Yonah and Zainam Higgins had Top 5 singles with 'Life Ain't Easy' and a cover of the Jackson 5 hit 'I Want You Back'. Under what name did they record these hits?

7 Apollo 440 had a Top 5 single with their theme tune to the film version of which sixties sci-fi TV series?

8 Can you name the lead singer and songwriter with The Lightning Seeds who, along with David Baddiel and Frank Skinner, reached number one for the second time with a re-recorded version of their song 'Three Lions'?

9 Alanis Morissette released the follow-up album to her multi-million selling *Jagged Little Pill* this year. What was it called?

10 Which American rapper featured alongside Melanie B on her number one debut solo hit 'I Want You Back'? (Not the same song as the one mentioned in Question 6!)

ANSWERS TO 1997

1. *Be Here Now* (Reportedly sold just a few thousand less than 700,000 copies in three days.) 2. Shola Ama (Her song 'You're The One I Love', had been released in 1996, but only became a Top 40 hit after the success of 'You Might Need Somebody'.) 3. 'You Can Leave Your Hat On' 4. Gala 5. 'Falling In Love (Is Hard On The Knees)' 6. Suggs 7. 'My Father's Son' 8. 911 9. *On Her Majesty's Secret Service* 10. David Bowie

1999

1. S Club 7 entered the chart at number one with their debut hit 'Bring It All Back', shortly after their debut TV series began on the BBC. What is the name of that TV series?

2. Which Canadian group reached the Top 3 with the song 'Drinking In L.A.'?

3. 'Maria' by Blondie was the group's first new hit song for seventeen years and first number one for nineteen years. They followed this with another Top 40 hit this year. What was it called?

4. Gregg Alexander and Danielle Brisebois were the key members of a short-lived American act who had a Top 5 single called 'You Get What You Give'. What is the name of the act?

5. Vengaboys number one 'We're Going To Ibiza!' was based on which 1975 number one hit?

6. Which American band made their only two UK chart appearances this year with the Top 5 song 'Kiss Me' and a Top 20 cover of The La's hit 'There She Goes'?

7 Beginning with the earliest, put these four songs in the order they were number one this year: 'Fly Away' by Lenny Kravitz, 'Lift Me Up' by Geri Halliwell, 'Sweet Like Chocolate' by Shanks & Bigfoot, 'When You Say Nothing At All' by Ronan Keating?

8 Elvis Costello reached the charts with his version of Charles Aznavour's number one 'She'. It featured on the soundtrack to a romantic comedy starring Julia Roberts and Hugh Grant. What was the film called?

9 The number one '9PM (Till I Come)' and its Top 3 follow-up 'Don't Stop' were both hits for the German DJ and producer André Tanneberger. Under what name did he record these tracks?

10 The final new number one of the nineties was a double A-side by an Irish group. Both songs were cover versions. What were the songs and which group recorded this double A-side?

ANSWERS TO 1998

1. 'Angels' 2. John Prescott 3. *Whistle Down The Wind* 4. Billie (Piper) with'Because We Want To' 5. Pras Michel with 'Ghetto Supastar (That Is What You Are)' 6. Cleopatra (They also had a Top 5 single called 'Cleopatra's Theme' this year.) 7. *Lost In Space* 8. Ian Broudie ('Three Lions' was originally number one in 1996 for Euro '96. It became number one again this year for the World Cup in France, billed as 'Three Lions '98'.) 9. *Supposed Former Infatuation Junkie* 10. Missy Elliott

BLUR

1. According to the title of the group's 1993 album, what do Blur consider *Modern Life* _____ to be?

2. Which member of Blur is also a cheesemaker?

3. The video for which of the band's singles features an animated walking milk carton?

4. Which artist and illustrator co-created the virtual band Gorillaz with Damon Albarn?

5. What was the group's only Top 40 hit of the 2010s?

6. Which actor speaks the verses of the 1994 Top 10 single 'Parklife'?

7 What type of '_____ Man' did Blur sing about on their 1996 Top 5 song?

8 Graham Coxon played guitars and co-wrote a number of the songs on the 2021 Top 3 album *Future Past*, the fifteenth studio album by one of the biggest bands of the eighties. What was the band called?

9 What is the one-word title of Blur's 1991 debut studio album?

10 Along with composer Ian Arber, which member of the band composed the music for the 2018 Bros documentary *Bros: After The Screaming Stops*?

ANSWERS TO 1999

1. *Miami 7* 2. Bran Van 3000 (The song had spent one week in the Top 40 the previous year when it was originally released. It was the group's only British hit song.) 3. 'Nothing Is Real But The Girl' 4. New Radicals 5. 'Barbados' by Typically Tropical 6. Sixpence None The Richer 7. 'Fly Away' (February), 'Sweet Like Chocolate' (May), 'When You Say Nothing At All' (August), 'Lift Me Up' (November) 8. *Notting Hill* 9. ATB 10. 'I Have A Dream' and 'Seasons In The Sun' by Westlife

CELINE DION

1. The 1997 Top 3 song 'Tell Him' was a duet between Celine and which legendary singer?

2. Her Top 5 single 'Because You Loved Me' was the theme from which 1996 movie starring Robert Redford and Michelle Pfeiffer?

3. Which country did Celine represent when she entered the Eurovision Song Contest in 1988 with the song '*Ne Partez Pas Sans Moi*'?

4. Originally a Top 20 hit for Roberta Flack in 1972, which song did Celine take back into the charts in 2000?

5. Which group both wrote and sang backing vocals on her 1998 Top 5 single 'Immortality'?

6. Although only a minor hit in the UK, what was the title of Celine's first American Top 5 hit?

7 Which legendary record producer was behind the controls of Celine's 1997 Top 20 single 'The Reason'?

8 Her 2003 album *One Heart* opens with her version of a song that had been a hit for both Cyndi Lauper and Roy Orbison. What is the song?

9 Who wrote her 1996 Top 3 single, 'It's All Coming Back To Me Now'?

10 In her first major film role, what is the title of the 2023 movie in which Celine appears as a fictional version of herself?

ANSWERS TO BLUR

1. *Modern Life is Rubbish* 2. Alex James 3. 'Coffee + TV' 4. Jamie Hewlett 5. 'Under The Westway' (lead track on a double A-side with 'The Puritan') 6. Phil Daniels 7. 'Charmless Man' 8. Duran Duran 9. *Leisure* 10. Dave Rowntree (as David Rowntree)

MARIAH CAREY

1. What was the title of Mariah's 1990 Top 10 debut hit?

2. Spending 16 weeks at the top of the American charts and a UK Top 10 hit, with which vocal group did she record the 1995 single 'One Sweet Day'?

3. What was the title of the 1999 movie starring Chris O'Donnell and Renée Zellweger that gave Mariah her first major big-screen role?

4. Although different songs, what one-word title is shared by a 1993 Top 10 hit for Mariah and a 2002 number one by Enrique Iglesias?

5. Her hit from 2000, 'Thank God I Found You' featuring Joe and 98 Degrees, was produced by Mariah with which two legendary song-writers and producers?

6. Who was the uncredited vocalist on Mariah's 1992 Top 3 single 'I'll Be There', recorded live for MTV's *Unplugged* series?

7 She had a Top 20 hit in 2009 with her version of a number one from the mid-eighties. What is that number one song and who sang the original?

8 In which year did her all-time bestselling Christmas song by a female artist, 'All I Want For Christmas Is You', first make the UK charts?

9 In 1998, Mariah and Whitney Houston recorded the duet 'When You Believe' for which animated movie?

10 In 2001, Mariah had a Top 10 album that was the soundtrack to a movie in which she starred. What was the title of both the album and movie?

ANSWERS TO CELINE DION

1. Barbra Streisand 2. 'Up Close And Personal' 3. Switzerland 4. 'The First Time Ever I Saw Your Face' 5. The Bee Gees (Billed as Celine Dion with special guests The Bee Gees) 6. 'Where Does My Heart Beat Now' 7. Sir George Martin (His son Giles Martin was assistant producer) 8. 'I Drove All Night' 9. Jim Steinman 10. 'Love Again'

OASIS

1. The group made its Top 40 debut in 1994 with which single?

2. Prior to being in Oasis, Noel Gallagher had been a roadie for which of these groups: Primal Scream, The Charlatans or Inspiral Carpets?

3. Billed as Oas*s, the record label Fierce Panda had a very minor hit in 1995 with a single featuring a 'conversation' between the Gallagher brothers. What was it called?

4. Who was the bass player in the band throughout the nineties?

5. In 1995, which single by the group was pitted against 'Country House' by Blur in what was called 'The Battle of Britpop'?

6 Which actor makes a guest appearance playing slide guitar on the track 'Fade In-Out' on the band's 1997 album *Be Here Now*?

7 Oasis released their first official live album in 2000. What is it called?

8 A cover of which number one by Slade featured on the CD single of 'Don't Look Back In Anger'?

9 Certified 11x platinum within a year of its release, which Welsh record producer co-produced *(What's The Story) Morning Glory*? with Noel Gallagher?

10 What is the title of Liam Gallagher's number one debut solo album, released in 2017?

ANSWERS TO MARIAH CAREY

1. 'Vision Of Love' 2. Boyz II Men 3. *The Bachelor* 4. 'Hero' 5. Jimmy Jam and Terry Lewis 6. Trey Lorenz 7. 'I Want To Know What Love Is' by Foreigner 8. 1994 9. *The Prince Of Egypt* 10. *Glitter*

SPICE GIRLS

1. What was the name of the 1997 film that starred all five girls along with Richard E. Grant, Meat Loaf and Roger Moore?

2. Counting double A-sides as one, how many number one hits did they achieve?

3. Just one of their releases between 1996 and 2000 didn't make it to number one. It entered the charts at its number two peak. What was it called, and for a bonus point what stopped it being number one?

4. Which member of the group landed parts in both *EastEnders* and *The Bill* prior to joining Spice Girls?

5. In 2004, Victoria Beckham reached the Top 3 with her double A-side single 'This Groove' and which other song?

6. Who had her first solo hit in 1999 with the Top 3 song 'Look At Me'?

7 Prior to being named Spice Girls, and when Michelle Stephenson was a member of the group, what name did they go under?

8 What was the title of the third Spice Girls' studio album that included the hits 'Holler' and 'Goodbye'?

9 At the height of their nineties fame, and again at their 2019 reunion tour, the group featured on packets of which brand of crisps?

10 The B-side of 'Spice Up Your Life' was recorded in a hurry when the girls were asked to talk about anything that came into their heads, then a backing track was added to this. What was the title of the track?

ANSWERS TO OASIS

1. 'Supersonic' 2. Inspiral Carpets 3. 'Wibbling Rivalry' 4. Paul McGuigan ('Guigsy') 5. 'Roll With It' 6. Johnny Depp 7. *Familiar To Millions* 8. 'Cum On Feel The Noize' 9. Owen Morris 10. *As You Were*

CHAMPIONS POPMASTER

Here we are at the business end of the book. Ten sets of questions of the standard played by the best of the best PopMaster contestants. There's only one point for each answer, with the exception of one question in each set, which is worth two points. If you play all ten rounds, will you score 110 out of 100?! Good luck!

CHAMPIONS 1

1 What is the title of the 2002 Top 10 duet by Russell Watson and Faye Tozer?

2 The songs 'Darling Pretty' in 1996 and 'Boom, Like That' in 2004 are the only two Top 40 solo singles by which singer and guitarist?

3 In 1969, The Beach Boys achieved their final hit of the sixties with which song?

4 Hot Chocolate's single 'Brother Louie' has been both a 1973 American number one for a rock band from New York City, and a 1993 Top 40 cover in the UK for a British rock band. **For two points**, can you name both bands?

5 What was the title of Kate Bush's residency at London's Hammersmith Apollo in 2014?

6 Released in 2006 and billed as just 'Alesha', Alesha Dixon had her debut solo hit with which song?

7 What do these four singers have in common: Tony Hadley, Wendy Page, Shelley Nelson and Espiritu?

8 The group Fat Larry's Band is best known for the 1982 Top 3 hit 'Zoom', but they had already had a Top 40 single in the seventies. What was that called?

9 Which boy band had Top 40 hits in the nineties with cover versions of 'Heaven Must Be Missing An Angel', 'Everlasting Love' and 'Could It Be I'm Falling In Love'?

10 José Feliciano had a Top 10 single in 1968 with 'Light My Fire'. The following year he had his only other Top 40 hit of the sixties. What was that called?

ANSWERS TO SPICE GIRLS

1. *Spice World* 2. Nine 3. 'Stop' (kept from being No. 1 by Run DMC vs Jason Nevins' 'It's Like That') 4. Emma Bunton 5. 'Let Your Head Go' 6. Geri Halliwell 7. Touch 8. *Forever* 9. Walkers 10. 'Spice Invaders'

CHAMPIONS 2

1. The Electric Light Orchestra had their last original Top 40 single in 1986. What was it called?

2. 'More Than I Needed To Know' was a Top 5 song in 2000 for which vocal pop group?

3. The Utah Saints' 1993 Top 10 single 'Believe In Me' contains portions of two Top 10 hits from the early eighties. **For two points**, can you name both of these hits and who recorded them?

4. Who duetted with Andy Williams on his 2002 version of 'Can't Take My Eyes Off You'?

5. Art Garfunkel has had three solo Top 40 hits during the seventies: the number ones 'I Only Have Eyes For You' and 'Bright Eyes', plus which other song?

6. What do these four chart acts have in common: Simon & Garfunkel, David Essex, Razorlight and The Nice?

7 The singers who didn't make it into the final selection for the boy band One True Voice on the TV show *Popstars: The Rivals* formed their own boy band and had four Top 40 hits in the noughties, including a cover of a Duran Duran song. What were they called and what was that Duran Duran cover?

8 Which American vocal group had a Top 40 hit in 1995 with The Eagles' song 'I Can't Tell You Why'?

9 In 1967, The Rolling Stones reached the Top 10 with their double A-side 'Dandelion' and which other song?

10 What do these four labels have in common: Gingerbread Man Records, Tennman Records, Unsub Records, Luaka Bop?

ANSWERS TO CHAMPIONS 1

1. 'Someone Like You' 2. Mark Knopfler 3. 'Break Away' 4. Stories (US No. 1 for two weeks in 1973), Quireboys (No. 32 in 1993) 5. 'Before The Dawn' 6. 'Lipstick' 7. They have all been featured vocalists on hit singles by Tin Tin Out 8. 'Center City' 9. Worlds Apart 10. 'And The Sun Will Shine'

CHAMPIONS 3

1 What song title has provided different Top 40 hits for The Detroit Spinners in 1980, Queen in 1982 and Adventures of Stevie V in 1990?

2 Who wrote Buddy Holly's 1959 posthumous number one 'It Doesn't Matter Anymore'?

3 What 2007 Top 10 single by Craig David includes a sample of David Bowie's 'Let's Dance'?

4 'Christmas Countdown' was a Top 40 hit in December 1983 for which Irish actor?

5 U2's thirteenth studio album was 2014's *Songs Of Innocence*. Their fourteenth was *Songs Of Experience* in 2017. What was the band's 2023 and fifteenth studio album called?

6 What do these four singles have in common: 'Can't Stand Losing You' by The Police, 'Hangin' Tough' by New Kids On The Block, 'Kings Of The Wild Frontier' by Adam and the Ants, 'Love Is A Stranger' by Eurythmics?

7 Having had hits with Split Enz, Crowded House and as Finn with his brother Tim, Neil Finn had his debut solo Top 40 single in 1998 with which song?

8 Two British versions of the song 'When My Little Girl Is Smiling' made the Top 10 in the early sixties. **For two points** can you name both singers?

9 Which 1984 Top 10 single by Kool & The Gang has the subtitle '(When You Say You Love Somebody)'?

10 Which British band had a Top 40 single in 1987 with their version of R. Dean Taylor's 1974 hit 'There's A Ghost In My House'?

ANSWERS TO CHAMPIONS 2

1. 'Calling America' 2. Scooch 3. 'Love Action (I Believe In Love)' by Human League, 'You Gave Me Love' by Crown Heights Affair (it also contained part of 'Do You Wanna Funk' by Sylvester, although this wasn't Top 10.) 4. Denise Van Outen 5. 'Since I Don't Have You' 6. Hit singles called 'America' (The Nice single combined part of Dvorak's *New World* symphony with 'America' from *West Side Story*.) 7. Phixx with 'Wild Boys' (They had four Top 40 hits, two more than One True Voice.) 8. Brownstone (written by Timothy B. Schmidt, Don Henley & Glenn Frey from the 1979 album *The Long Run*) 9. 'We Love You' 10. They are all labels that were founded or co-founded by artists: Ed Sheeran; Justin Timberlake; Katy Perry (originally called Metamorphosis Music); David Byrne

CHAMPIONS 4

1 The song 'Only Happy When it Rains' in 1995 was the first Top 40 single for which group?

2 Carl Douglas followed up his 1974 number one 'Kung Fu Fighting' with a Top 40 single that also had a martial arts title. What was it?

3 Five Star had fifteen Top 40 hits in the eighties. They were all members of the Pearson family: Denise, Stedman, Doris, Delroy and ____ who?

4 What was the title of the only hit by Freddy Cannon to make the Top 10 in the sixties?

5 A version of Roy Orbison's 'Blue Bayou' was a 1978 Top 40 hit for which American singer?

6 John Parr, who had a Top 10 hit in 1985 with 'St Elmo's Fire (Man In Motion)' was a guest vocalist on a 1986 Top 40 single by Meat Loaf. What was it called?

7 The song 'This Summer' reached the Top 40 in 1995 and then again as a remix in 1996 for which group?

8 *Life In Cartoon Motion* was the title of Mika's 2007 number one album. What was the title of his 2009 Top 10 follow-up?

9 Which legendary singer topped the album charts for seven weeks in 1957 with *A Swingin' Affair*?

10 **For two points**, what comes next (and last) in this sequence and what is the connection: 'Pillowtalk', 'This Town', 'Just Hold On', 'Sign Of The Times'...?

ANSWERS TO CHAMPIONS 3

1. 'Body Language' 2. Paul Anka 3. 'Hot Stuff (Let's Dance)' 4. Frank Kelly (who would go on to play Father Jack in *Father Ted*) 5. *Songs Of Surrender* (Features re-recorded versions of songs throughout the band's career.) 6. Although all were released first, they all became the second Top 40 hit for each act (Police No. 42 in 1978, No. 2 in 1979 following the release of 'Roxanne'; New Kids on the Block No. 52 in 1989, No. 1 in 1990 following the release of 'You Got It (The Right Stuff)'; Adam and the Ants No. 48 in 1980, No. 2 in 1981 following the release of 'Dog Eat Dog'; Eurythmics No. 54 in 1982, No. 6 in 1983 following the release of 'Sweet Dreams (Are Made Of This)'.) 7. 'She Will Have Her Way' 8. Jimmy Justice and Craig Douglas (both versions were in the chart at the same time in 1962) 9. '(When You Say You Love Somebody) In The Heart' 10. The Fall

CHAMPIONS 5

1. Having entered the charts in December 2019, which song by The Weeknd spent a total of eight weeks at number one in 2020?

2. Which hit group of the early eighties had a lead singer called Mike Score?

3. What '_____ River' did The Brecker Brothers sing about on their 1978 Top 40 hit?

4. Who made her final Top 40 appearance of the 20th century in 1990 with the song 'Reputation'?

5. 'Hayseeds Sated Sociopaths' is an anagram of two number one singles: one from 1975, the other from 1980. **For two points**, what are the titles of the number ones and what is the connection?

6. A 1961 number one by The Highwaymen and a 2004 Top 20 single by Franz Ferdinand share the same one-word title. What is that title?

7 What connects these four singles in the seventies: 'Hey Rock and Roll', 'You Just Might See Me Cry', 'Sad Sweet Dreamer', 'Milky Way'?

8 In between Elvis Presley in 1969 and Fine Young Cannibals in 1986, one other chart act had a Top 40 hit with the song 'Suspicious Minds'. Who was it?

9 In the mid-nineties, Rednex followed up the number one 'Cotton Eye Joe' with which Top 20 single?

10 Which duo reached the Top 20 in 2000 with a cover of Alice Cooper's number one 'School's Out'?

ANSWERS TO CHAMPIONS 4

1. Garbage 2. 'Dance The Kung Fu' (No. 35 in 1974) 3. Lorraine 4. 'Way Down Yonder In New Orleans' 5. Linda Ronstadt 6. 'Rock 'n' Roll Mercenaries' 7. Squeeze 8. *The Boy Who Knew Too Much* 9. Frank Sinatra 10. 'Strip That Down' – these were the debut chart appearances by the five original members of One Direction outside of the group (Zayn Malik, Niall Horan, Louis Tomlinson & Steve Aoki, Harry Styles, Liam Payne featuring Quavo)

CHAMPIONS 6

1 What is the connection between 'I'm A Man', 'More Than A Feeling', 'Dr Beat' and 'I'm Doing Fine Now'?

2 What shared song title has provided both Sad Cafe with a Top 40 hit in 1980 and The Stranglers with a different Top 10 single in 1982?

3 Under what name did Colin Blunstone record his 1969 solo version of the Zombies' hit 'She's Not There'?

4 Paolo Nutini made his chart debut in 2006 with which Top 5 song?

5 Jermaine Stewart had his third and final original Top 40 hit in 1988 with a song that has the same title as a 2013 month-long number one. What is that shared title?

6 Can you name the singer-songwriter who topped the album charts in 1965 with *Bringing It All Back Home*?

7 Beginning with 'Call It Love' and ending with 'No Surrender', the vocal pop group Deuce had four Top 40 hits in the nineties. Can you name one of the two in between?

8 Daniel Boone had hits in the seventies with 'Beautiful Sunday' and 'Daddy Don't You Walk So Fast'. **For two points**, by what other name was he better known for his songwriting skills?

9 Kelly Marie, who reached number one in 1980 with 'Feels Like I'm In Love', went on to have two further Top 40 solo hits. Can you name either of these?

10 The song 'Hold Onto Our Love' was both a Top 20 single and the UK's Eurovision entry in 2004. Who sang it?

ANSWERS TO CHAMPIONS 5

1. 'Blinding Lights' 2. A Flock Of Seagulls 3. 'East River' 4. Dusty Springfield 5. 'Space Oddity' and 'Ashes To Ashes' are both number ones by David Bowie that mention the character Major Tom. 6. 'Michael' 7. Debut chart hits of groups that had appeared on the talent show *New Faces* (Showaddywaddy, Our Kid, Sweet Sensation, Sheer Elegance). 8. Candi Staton (Top 40 in 1982) 9. 'Old Pop In An Oak' 10. Daphne & Celeste

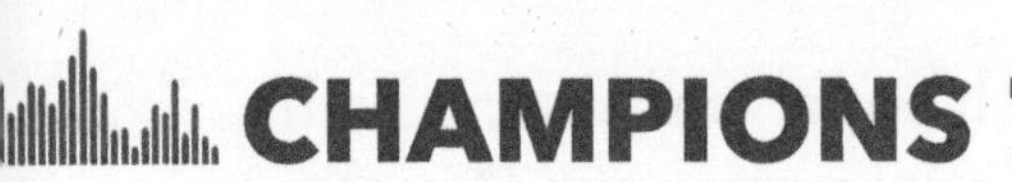

CHAMPIONS 7

1. What one-word song title has provided different Top 40 hits for George Harrison, S Club 7 and Bonnie Raitt?

2. 'Ceremony' is the title of the 1981 chart debut by which group?

3. 'Stuck In The Middle With You' and 'Star' were the first and last of three Top 40 singles by Stealers Wheel. What is the title of the one that came in between?

4. Which football club has had Top 40 hits called 'Here We Go' in 1985 and 'All Together Now' in 1995?

5. Released in 2013, what was the title of David Bowie's first Top 10 hit for twenty years?

6. Who had a Top 20 hit in 1962 with the song 'Will I What' and, **for two points**, who was the female guest replying to the vocalist?

7 What shared song title has provided different Top 10 hits for Steps in 1998 and a Ronan Keating/Leann Rimes duet in 2004?

8 Apart from all having female members, what do these four groups specifically have in common: Voice Of The Beehive, Heart, The Bangles, B*Witched?

9 The group Goodbye Mr. Mackenzie made its only Top 40 appearance in 1989 with which single?

10 Which member of the vocal group Eternal had a solo hit in 1999 called 'Higher Than Heaven'?

ANSWERS TO CHAMPIONS 6

1. Debut Top 40 hits by groups that all have American cities in their names (Chicago, Boston, Miami Sound Machine, New York City). 2. 'Strange Little Girl' 3. Neil MacArthur 4. 'Last Request' 5. 'Get Lucky' (The 2013 No. 1 was by Daft Punk with Pharrell Williams and Nile Rodgers. Jermaine's debut hit 'We Don't Have To Take Our Clothes Off' reached the Top 40 again in 2011.) 6. Bob Dylan 7. 'I Need You' (Top 10 in 1995), 'On The Bible' (Top 20 in 1995) 8. Peter Lee Stirling (born Peter Green) 9. 'Loving Just For Fun' (Top 40 in '80), 'Hot Love' (Top 40 in '81) 10. James Fox

CHAMPIONS 8

1 What shared one-word song title has provided different Top 40 hits for Earth Wind & Fire in the seventies, Gerard Kenny in the eighties, Mariah Carey in the nineties and Appleton in the noughties?

2 Who or what links these early eighties hits: 'Banana Republic' by The Boomtown Rats, 'Show Me' by Dexy's Midnight Runners', 'Will You?' by Hazel O'Connor and 'Best Years Of Our Lives' by Modern Romance?

3 The band A1 had both of their number one singles in 2000. The first was a cover of a-ha's 'Take On Me'. What was the second?

4 Prior to her solo career, Sophie Ellis-Bextor had hit singles in 1998 as the lead singer of which group?

5 Legendary jazz singer Ella Fitzgerald reached the Top 40 in 1964 with her version of which Beatles hit?

6 Which country singer is billed alongside Nelly on his 2005 number one 'Over And Over'?

7 Three chart acts had Top 40 hits in the 20th century with different songs called 'All Fall Down'. Five Star is one. **For two points**, can you name one of the other two?

8 The Italian singer Drupi made his only UK chart appearance in 1973 with which Top 40 song?

9 Which two Motown acts joined forces on the 1969 hit 'I Second That Emotion', a year after the song had reached the charts for Smokey Robinson & The Miracles?

10 Released in 2019, the combined talents of Stormzy, Ed Sheeran and Burna Boy spent three weeks at number one in 2020 with which song?

ANSWERS TO CHAMPIONS 7

1. 'You' 2. New Order 3. 'Everything Will Turn Out Fine' (some copies printed as 'Everything'll Turn Out Fine') 4. Everton ('Here We Go' billed as Everton 1985, 'All Together Now' billed as Everton Football Club.) 5. 'Where Are We Now?' 6. Mike Sarne with Billie Davis 7. 'Last Thing On My Mind' 8. Each group contains a pair of sisters (Tracy Bryn and Melissa Brooke Belland, Ann and Nancy Wilson, Debbi and Vicki Peterson, Edele and Keavy Lynch) 9. 'The Rattler' 10. Kéllé Bryan

CHAMPIONS 9

1 The Fatback Band had a hit with '(Do The) Spanish Hustle' in 1976, but which group had a Top 10 hit with 'British Hustle' in 1978?

2 Adamski followed up his 1990 number one 'Killer' with his only other Top 10 single. What was it called?

3 Who had a number one album in 2007 called *All The Lost Souls*?

4 What's the connection between 'Delirious', 'Incredible', 'Superficial', 'Complicated'?

5 Which famous guitarist joined Bryan Ferry's band at Live Aid in 1985, playing a solo on 'Slave To Love'?

6 '(Irish Wolfy Witherman)' is an anagram of the five-word subtitle to a 2006 number one. **For two points**, what is the full title of that number one and who recorded it?

7 Which singing actor had hits in the early sixties with 'Wild Wind', 'Son, This Is She' and 'Lonely City'?

8 The Mavericks followed up their 1998 Top 5 hit 'Dance The Night Away' with the band's only other Top 40 single. It was called 'I've Got _____' what?

9 Released in 1976, what was the first Top 40 hit by Fleetwood Mac to feature Lindsey Buckingham and Stevie Nicks in the group's line-up?

10 Which jazz-funk group played horns on Spandau Ballet's 1981 single 'Chant No. 1 (I Don't Need This Pressure On)' and had their own Top 40 hits that year with '(Somebody) Help Me Out' and 'Mule (Chant No. 2)'?

ANSWERS TO CHAMPIONS 8

1. 'Fantasy' (Earth Wind & Fire reached No. 14 in 1978, Gerard Kenny No. 34 in 1980, Mariah Carey No. 4 in 1995, Appleton No. 2 in 2002.) 2. They were all produced by Tony Visconti. 3. 'Same Old Brand New You' 4. Theaudience 5. 'Can't Buy Me Love' 6. Tim McGraw 7. Lindisfarne (1972) and Ultravox (1986) 8. 'Vado Via' 9. Diana Ross & The Supremes and The Temptations 10. 'Own It'

CHAMPIONS 10

1. What comes next: Grand Piano, Reed & Pipe Organ, Glockenspiel, Bass Guitar, _____ what?

2. Amy Grant, who had a Top 3 hit in 1991 with the song 'Baby, Baby' had two other Top 40 singles that decade. Name either of them?

3. What shared two-word song title has provided different Top 40 hits for both SWV and Ultimate Kaos in the nineties and both Jess Glynne and Rudimental featuring Foxes in the 2010s?

4. The 1989 song 'The Message Is Love' was a Top 40 hit for Arthur Baker and the Backbeat Disciples, featuring which soul singer?

5. What three words were in brackets at the end of Cliff Richard's 1965 Top 3 hit 'Wind Me Up'?

6. Who represented the UK at Eurovision in 2008 with the song 'Even If'?

7 Which singer recorded the 1977 duet 'You Take My Heart Away' with DeEtta Little?

8 In 1987, Sam Moore and Lou Reed reached the Top 40 with the version of a song Moore had originally recorded with Dave Prater for a hit in 1967. What is the song?

9 The songs 'When Do I Get To Sing 'My Way'' and 'When I Kiss You (I Hear Charlie Parker Playing)' were Top 40 hits in the mid-nineties for which chart act?

10 'Hateful Merrielle Regurgitates' is an anagram of three glam rock hits, one each from Mud, Sweet and T.Rex. **For two points**, work out the three songs, then, beginning with the earliest, put them in the order they were originally hits.

ANSWERS TO CHAMPIONS 9

1. Hi Tension 2. 'The Space Jungle' 3. James Blunt 4. The things 'She Is...,' according to Ottawan's 'D.I.S.C.O.' 5. David Gilmour 6. 'I Wish I Was A Punk Rocker (With Flowers In My Hair)' by Sandi Thom 7. John Leyton (He also had a No. 1 in 1961 with 'Johnny Remember Me'.) 8. 'I've Got This Feeling' 9. 'Say You Love Me' (lead vocal by Christine McVie, who wrote the song) 10. Beggar and Co.

ONE YEAR OUT!

Surely you didn't think there could be a PopMaster book without a set of these?!?

Every competitor playing the quiz on Ken's radio show gets a 'guess the year' question. We've saved it till the end, so can you guess the year for each of these months? Will you be spot on? Or will you be one year out?

ONE YEAR OUT!

The 'nemesis' question for so many playing on air. Can you guess the years in question for the following months.

1. **JANUARY** – In which year did these three songs all enter the Top 40 in this month: 'Relax Take It Easy' by Mika, 'Piece Of Me' by Britney Spears and 'Chasing Pavements' by Adele?

2. **FEBRUARY** – In which year did these three songs all enter the Top 40 in this month: 'Street Spirit (Fade Out)' by Radiohead, 'Children' by Robert Miles and 'One Of Us' by Joan Osborne?

3. **MARCH** – In which year did these three songs all enter the Top 40 in this month: 'Spanish Wine' by Chris White, 'I'm Mandy, Fly Me' by 10cc and 'You See The Trouble With Me' by Barry White?

4 **APRIL** – In which year did these three songs all enter the Top 40 in this month: 'A Little Bit Me, A Little Bit You' by The Monkees, 'Dedicated To The One I Love' by The Mamas and The Papas and 'Hi Ho Silver Lining' by Jeff Beck?

5 **MAY** – In which year did these three songs all enter the Top 40 in this month: 'I'm With Stupid' by Pet Shop Boys, 'Fill My Little World' by The Feeling and 'Lost & Found' by Feeder?

6 **JUNE** – In which year did these three songs all enter the Top 40 in this month: 'Never Really Over' by Katy Perry, 'Heaven' by Avicii and 'You Need To Calm Down' by Taylor Swift?

7 **JULY** – In which year did these three songs all enter the Top 40 in this month: 'Down On The Street' by Shakatak, 'Eyes Without A Face' by Billy Idol and 'Come Back' by The Mighty Wah!?

8 **AUGUST** – In which year did these three songs all enter the Top 40 in this month: 'One In Ten' by UB40, 'The Thin Wall' by Ultravox and 'She's Got Claws' by Gary Numan?

9 **SEPTEMBER** – In which year did these three songs all enter the Top 40 in this month: 'Summer Night City' by ABBA, 'Ever Fallen In Love (With Someone You Shouldn't've)' by The Buzzcocks and 'Now That We've Found Love' by Third World?

10 **OCTOBER** – In which year did these three songs all enter the Top 40 in this month: 'Real Life' by Simple Minds, 'Go' by Moby and 'This House' by Alison Moyet?

11 **NOVEMBER** – In which year did these three songs all enter the Top 40 in this month: 'Candy' by Robbie Williams, 'I Found You' by The Wanted and 'DNA' by Little Mix?

12 **DECEMBER** – In which year did these three songs all enter the Top 30 in this month: 'Deck Of Cards' by Wink Martindale, 'Little White Bull' by Tommy Steele and 'Among My Souvenirs' by Connie Francis?

ANSWERS TO CHAMPIONS 10

1. Double Speed Guitar (The instruments, in chronological order from the start, introduced by Vivian Stanshall as 'Master Of Ceremonies' in part 1 of 'Tubular Bells'.) 2. 'Every Heartbeat' (1991), 'Big Yellow Taxi' (Joni Mitchell cover 1995) 3. 'Right Here' 4. Al Green 5. '(Let Me Go)' 6. Andy Abraham 7. Nelson Pigford 8. 'Soul Man' 9. Sparks 10. 'Metal Guru' (1972), 'Hellraiser' (1973), 'Tiger Feet' (1974)

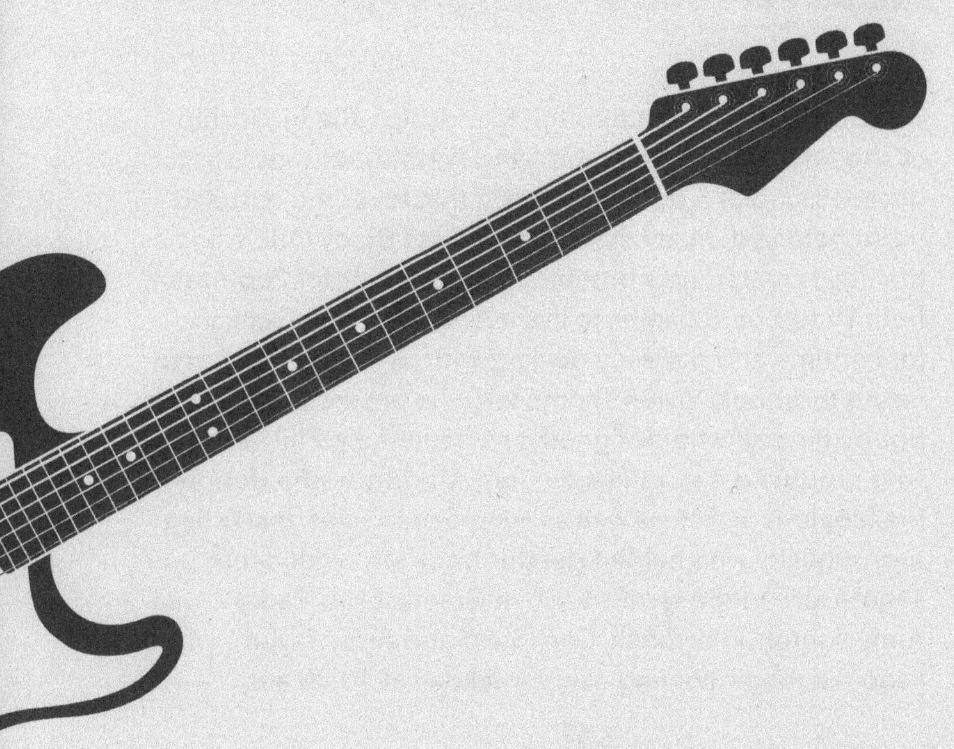

ANSWERS TO ONE YEAR OUT!

1. 2008 (Mika originally released in 2007, but didn't reach the Top 40 until 2008) 2. 1996 3. 1976 4. 1967 5. 2006 6. 2019 7. 1984 8. 1981 9. 1978 10. 1991 11. 2012 12. 1959

ACKNOWLEDGEMENTS

This book came about through friendship – the friendship of a team that has been producing PopMaster questions for decades, and of a publishing team that loves the quiz and those behind it. Many thanks to Vanessa Brady OBE who has tirelessly created new business opportunities for PopMaster, from TV to board games to live events. To Steph Duncan for her time and patience dealing with us all and helping to create this book, Vivien Thompson who ensured its accuracy, Bobby Birchall who designed it so beautifully, Phil Evans who produced it so brilliantly, Tony Maddock who designed the fabulous jacket, as well as everyone in sales, marketing and publicity who helped get this book into your hands. Thanks also to the terrific team at Greatest Hits Radio – Andy Ashton, David Salt, Gary Stein and Andy Taylor – who keep the magic coming every weekday at 10.30 am.

From Phil, a special thanks to my wife Lyndsey for her inspiration and putting up with all the time I spent in my office working on questions.

From Neil, this is for my late dad, an excellent musician who loved the operatic section of 'Bohemian Rhapsody' but not the 'racket' that followed it!

The final word of thanks must of course go to Ken Bruce, who has kept the PopMaster audience engaged for all these years with many more to come and last, but most certainly not least, our ever-loyal PopMaster audience. 'Keep On Keeping On'!

Picture Acknowledgements

Images © Shutterstock.

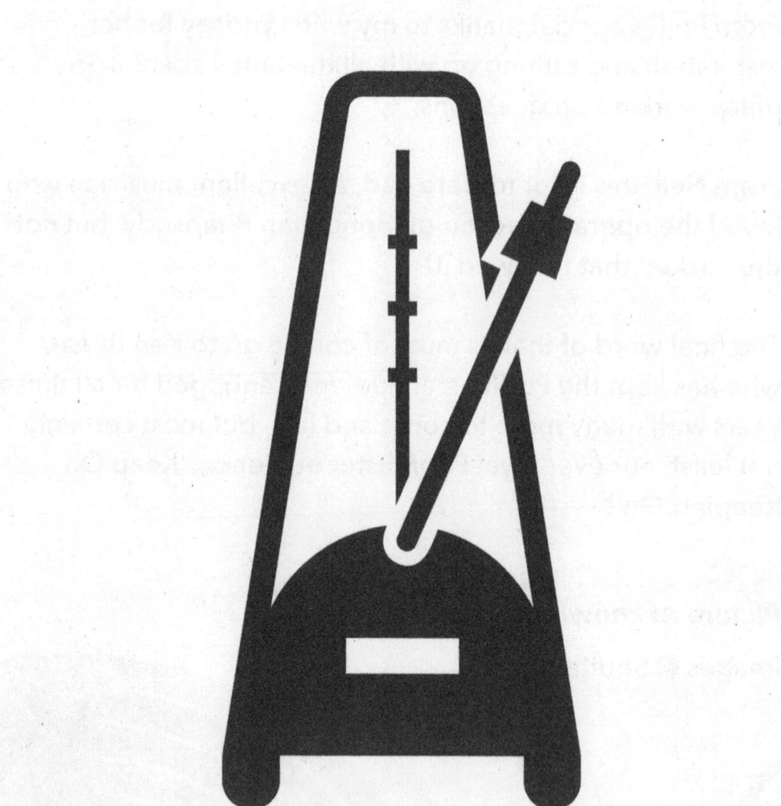